WHAT'S SO FUNNY?
THEORIES OF COMEDY

Stephen Hoover

What's So Funny? Theories of Comedy

Copyright © 2013 by Stephen Hoover

Library of Congress Control Number: 2013922637

Book design by: Cat Stewart

Cover design by: 2Faced Design

ISBN: 978-0-9897465-8-8

Dedicated to author Joe Adamson whose books inspired me to think seriously about comedy while making me laugh.

Table of Contents

Introduction:

What is funny to you? Why *doesn't* your mother think it is funny, and why does she look at you like that when you laugh at it? Does your spouse roll their, eyes and groan when you tell what you believe passes for a joke? You might be sitting there right now wondering if it is funny or if you have a few wires crossed in your brain. It might even be the reason you are reading this book.

Humor is a strange beast that can be very difficult to wrangle and define. If you ask many people, including comedians who work in the trade professionally, you *can't really* define humor and put it into a nice neat package that everyone can understand.

Hard to Define

All cultures on the planet have their own brand of humor and their own things that they think are funny. The people of Papua New Guinea have their type of humor that differs from what Canadians will probably find funny. The cultures don't have to be that far apart and disparate to have differences in humor, though. Consider the United States and the United Kingdom. The *brands* of humor are very different. Yet, there is some crossover, and both are highly funny. Still, some Americans don't *get* British humor and vice versa.

In This Book

What will you learn from reading this book? We'll do our very best to pull back the curtain and shine a light on humor and comedy, but it won't be easy. Humor is different things to different people, and that can make it elusive to grasp.

What you should ultimately take away from the book, though, is that your idea of comedy is not wrong. You have your own unique sense of humor, and that's a great thing.

You might like pratfalls and slapstick. That's a perfectly good and real type of comedy. Or, you might prefer cerebral comedy that requires in-depth knowledge of obscure world facts and you have the super-powered ability to withstand the whine of Dennis Miller. Maybe you like observational humor or anecdotal humor. Maybe you are a fan of puns. Perhaps you like it all.

In this book, we'll look at different types of comedy, theories of comedy from philosophers and researchers, the techniques of writing comedy, and much more. By the end, you should have a much better grasp of what comedy is and even how to create it. You will even have access to a glossary that will give you some definitions and examples of comedy theories and styles at a glance.

It's time to start having some fun!

Chapter 1

Why Do We *Need* to Laugh?

Y ou've heard plenty of people say that laughter is the best medicine, but it might be more than just a clichéd phrase. Laughter is fun, it makes us happy, and it is something we should all do more of each day. We all know this from experience. Watching a favorite sitcom or stand-up comedian can have us in stitches, and we always feel great afterward.

However, there are some legitimate medical reasons laughter is so good. Before we get into the mechanics of comedy and what makes us laugh, it's a good idea to know just why it is a good idea to keep laughing.

Decrease Your Stress

In today's busy world, stress affects us all. With kids preparing for tests at school, adults who worry about paying the bills on time, and everyone wondering about the economy and the security of their jobs, it is easy to see just how much we all "stress out" on a daily basis. We become shuddering pressure cookers that might just blow their tops if we aren't careful. We need some relief, and that's where comedy can come in, slip on a banana peel, and decrease that pressure.

When we laugh, our body goes through hormonal changes. We have decreases in the levels of epinephrine and cortisol, two stress hormones that affect us. When you feel a bit stressed, watch or read something funny and see how much better you feel.

Learn to Cope Better

In addition to helping with stress, laughter can help us cope with the bad parts of life. This ties in nicely to the ability of laughter to reduce your stress. When life keeps tossing problems and tragedies your way, simply laughing in the face of it is the best way to deal with the situation and keep your sanity.

You can't control all of the things that are happening in your world no matter how hard you try. However, you have control over how you react to the situation. Laughter can be a good way to cope even in the darkest of times.

When bad things happen, look to the lighter side when you can. If there was a death in the family, think of the happier times and the funny times with that person. Doing so will help to make it possible to deal with the tragedy. In fact, some therapists are starting to use laughter therapy as part of their treatment.

It's Like Exercise... Sort of

Are you running low on time? Can't get to the gym today? Why not do a few sets of laughter instead? While it might not be the same as an intense session on the elliptical trainer or with the free weights, you will find that laugher can actually offers some benefits similar to exercise.

Research shows that laughter can be quite effective. In fact, they say that laughing 100 times is about the same as spending ten minutes on a rowing machine or fifteen minutes on a stationary bike. Go spend an hour or two at the local comedy club and drop some pounds – well, as long as you have light beer or diet soda for your two-drink minimum.

Improve Your Blood Pressure
A study conducted at the University of Maryland showed that laughter and heart health had a link. According to the study, laughing can help to expand the tissue in the lining of the blood vessels. This allows the blood to flow better, and this means that it can reduce the blood pressure and make your heart healthier.

Can laughter help your heart? It's possible. Should you stop taking your heart medication and instead spend your money on DVD sets of *The Big Bang Theory*, *It's Always Sunny in Philadelphia*, *30 Rock*, and whatever else you find funny? No, you *really* do need to listen to your doctor. However, you can supplement your actual medical treatment with some laughter. Take two comedians and call us in the morning.

Squash Your Aggression
You can't get angry if you are laughing. Laughter can help to release the negative emotions you are holding inside, whether it is anger, fear, or aggression. Laughter releases those emotions in a positive manner. It all goes back to reducing stress, really. Now, if only Bruce Banner had learned about this benefit of comedy, he might never have had to rampage as the Hulk!

Improves the Immune System
You can actually have a nice boost to your immune system as well. Thanks to the decrease in the stress hormones and the better circulation and blood flow, not to mention the greater oxygen intake that happens with laughter, it's easy to see how laughing can make you a healthier and happier person.

Learn to Laugh

Is laughter magical? While it isn't a cure-all, it is good for you, and it is important to understand that when you start diving into the mechanisms that go into making comedy and the reasons we humans find certain things funny.

One of the interesting things we find, though, is that people often find different things funny. Even though the result of the laughter is the same on a chemical and emotional level in the body, it seems that humor can come from a variety of different places.

A number of different things can determine what makes people laugh, including their culture and upbringing and their peers. However, very young children all seem to take great pleasure in similar types of humor; mainly, they seem to enjoy surprises and the unexpected. As you will see, adults enjoy this as well, although our level of comedic sophistication is much higher... usually.

Throughout the rest of the book, we will examine some of the different theories of comedy, so we will have a better idea of what makes people laugh. We'll also look at works of humor throughout history, including quite a bit of modern comedy, to attempt to narrow down just why we laugh at certain things.

Chapter 2

What is Comedy?

The question that makes up the title of this chapter is something that's almost impossible to answer. Humor, like so many things in life, really is subjective. As mentioned in the last chapter, different people find different things funny. Different strokes for different folks, or as the theme song from the '80s sitcom so aptly put it, "It takes different strokes to rule the world."

Yes, it does, and in this chapter and the subsequent chapters of the book, really, we'll look at those different strokes. This chapter will scratch the surface; the others will cut deeper.

So, let's get into it. What is comedy? What makes things funny?

Comedy is Art and Art is – *Wait for It* – Subjective

Since there is so much subjectivity, it is important to cover as many different aspects and types of comedy as possible. Some things make us smile and laugh, and feel great. Others make us cringe and laugh, such as the antics of one Steve Carell's Michael Scott on the U.S.

version of *The Office* or Ricky Gervais' David Brent in the U.K. version. They are part of a long line of cringe-worthy comedy.

In this chapter, we will cover the basics of what constitutes comedy of different sorts and what makes us laugh.

One of the things that you want to remember is that if you overanalyze comedy, it can lose the humor. It's similar to learning how a magician performs feats of mysticism. As soon as you know how the magician does the trick, it really can strip away some of the magic. Analyzing is good – overanalyzing is bad. Of course, that's probably true of anything.

Comedy encompasses surprises, it captures moments of unexpectedness, and it can make us convulse with laughter. One of the simplest and purposefully obtuse ways to "define" comedy is that you know it when you see/hear it.

How do you know? Well, the biggest clue would be the fact that you are laughing! At the very least, humor will make you chuckle inwardly and perhaps shake your head.

The Link Between Comedy and Horror/Tragedy

Comedy is full of opposites, contradictions, callbacks, and tragedy. Comedy and tragedy, and even horror, have a very tight relationship built on tension and release of that tension. If you ever doubt that laughter and horror have a link, think about the folks who go to haunted houses every Halloween so they can pay to have people in costume scare the jeepers out of them.

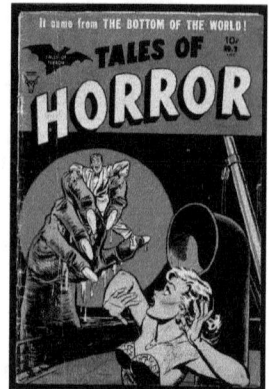

It came from THE BOTTOM OF THE WORLD!

TALES OF HORROR

Fear and Laughter

What so often happens in these places is that the fear turns into laughter. Sometimes it is giddy, uncontrollable, jabbering laughter, but regardless, fear – controlled fear at least tends to hit some of the *same* internal buttons that comedy does.

You can often feel this when you are watching horror movies as well, or even playing hide and seek as a child. How often did you find a great hiding place and then have to bite the inside of your cheek to keep from giggling as the person tasked with finding you walked past you? Again, it's a mingling of laughter and fear.

The exploration of both horror and comedy takes pain and tragedy and makes it easier to deal with them through cathartic release. They help people to face those fears and painful truths and learn to cope with them.

Maybe hitting someone in the face with a pie doesn't have the same effect, but the best of comedy *can* achieve this catharsis. That's why most comedians feel that there should be very few, if any taboos, when it comes to topics for comedy.

Maybe there's even a connection as to why clowns are funny to some and scary to others!

Examples of Horror/Comedy on the Screen

If you are still on the fence and wondering what monsters have to do with laughter, it's time we looked at some examples from the movies. Here are some comedy/horror gems.

Abbot and Costello Meet Frankenstein

Shaun of the Dead

Gremlins

Tucker & Dale vs Evil

Fright Night

Zombieland

Young Frankenstein

Slither

The Frighteners

Rocky Horror Picture Show

Ghostbusters

Once Bitten

Arachnophobia

Army of Darkness

Bubba Ho-Tep

These are fifteen of the best and funniest horror comedy films out there today and these movies just scratch the surface. Even when you look at serious horror films, you will notice how they often use comedic elements to change or redirect the feeling of tension in the film.

A bit of light comedy can put people off guard, and that's when they deliver the scare, the horror equivalent of a punch line. Think about one of the most overused devices in those types of films. Everything looks like the big scare is coming, only to find out that it was just that darned old cat.

Each of the movies depicted above uses comedy in different ways too. They embrace tropes, turn tropes on their head, and sometimes go for slapstick when the script calls for it.

Watch some of the above films and see how they weave comic elements, including dark comic elements, into the stories. Doing so will help you to see the relation between horror and comedy, and thus it can elevate your understanding of the theory of comedy.

Chew on this, too. One of the most popular television shows currently running is *The Walking Dead*. While you won't find too much humor in the show itself, a companion show called *The Talking Dead* is on right after it. Hosted by popular comedian Chris

Hardwick, the show features celebrity guests who are fans of *The Walking Dead*.

Hardwick's show always includes heaping doses of humor, despite the tragic nature of the show it covers. Once again, you can easily see that strong Fixodent-like bond between horror and humor.

Stand-Up Comedians Play with Tragedy and Comedy Too

It works in movies and on television, it works in writing, and it can work in stand-up comedy as well. One of the sayings is that tragedy plus time equals comedy. It is very true.

Watch most comedians today, such as Louis C.K. and Bill Burr, and you can see this intimate relationship between comedy and tragedy threaded through much of their acts.

It's Not All Doom and Gloom in Comedy

Thus far, it might seem like comedy is no laughing matter. Horror and tragedy aren't the only things that contribute to humor, though – not by a long shot. In addition, humor can come from varying degrees of tragedy.

Forgetting your umbrella when it starts to rain or slipping on a banana peel is different from death, of course. Yet, comedy can come from all of those things and so much more. It doesn't have to be doom and gloom, but there generally does have to be *some* element of loss or tragedy, however minor, for there to be humor.

This isn't *always* the case, but you will find it repeatedly with successful comedians and comedic bits. The brilliant and acerbic show *South Park* is a prime example of this. They find the humor in the unlikeliest of places. Some people believe they go too far on occasion, but most understand the goal of Parker and Stone's humor is to make one think and even question why they are laughing. As silly as many people might feel *South Park* is, it truly is one of the best, most biting comedies on television today.

Everything Is Funny

Do you remember when we said that everyone finds different things funny? You should, because it was just a few pages ago, and because it's entirely true. Everyone's sense of humor is unique, and that can make it difficult to boil it all down to "this is funny" and "that is funny," but "that is not funny." Some people laugh at highbrow humor from the New Yorker, and some laugh at farts. In fact, someone out there just giggled because he or she read the word farts.

Keep in mind too that many people will simply not be able to get on board with certain ideas regarding comedy. Some of the topics covered by South Park, for example, really are considered taboo and bad taste for many people.

The key to really understanding comedy is in trying to understand that different people laugh at different things and then to accept that. Once you accept it, you can really start to learn more about why some things are funny.

Wait, What's So Funny?

Let's look at why some things are funny. Sometimes they are funny because the joke or the story does something completely unexpected. Other times it's funny because the comedy follows the exact pattern you would expect from the logical progression of the joke. Even when something expected happens, the tension of getting there can be great for comedy. Sometimes it is familiar. Sometimes it is unfamiliar.

Often, it is funny because it is the *opposite* of what you feel will happen, even when it follows the conventional route. Does this sound confusing to you? It can be. Do you see a pattern here though? It was the best of times, it was the worst of times, it was the age of wisdom, it was the age of foolishness, and so on.

Dickens understood, even though *A Tale of Two Cities* isn't really sitcom material. So did Paula Abdul – opposites attract. Comedy is about opposites, it's about the unexpected, it is about uncomfortable situations. The play and television show *The Odd Couple* springs to mind here.

Yes, many different things are funny. Now we will start to look at some of the "tools of comedy" in order to understand how comedians, writers, and even life in general, can make things funny.

Knock, Knock, I Have a Delivery

A good joke requires a number of different things in order to be successful, and one of the most important of those things is the delivery. The delivery is simply the way that you tell a joke. Different people have different types of delivery. Hmm, that sounds remarkably similar to what we learned above – different people have different tastes in comedy.

The comedian's delivery develops over time in most cases. They will make their delivery a part of their personality.

What's in the Delivery?

Some comics, such as Dane Cook, are highly animated and sometimes bordering on frantic when they tell their jokes and stories. Others have a very subdued and laid-back delivery to their jokes. Look at popular comedians such as Stephen Wright and Brian Posehn to see some good examples of the relaxed and somewhat subdued delivery.

To get a good feel for the different styles of delivery, it's a good idea to look at the stand-up routines of several different comedians. Here are ten who have, by all accounts, excellent albeit different types of delivery.

Are these the only comedians you should watch? No, of course not, that would be silly. However, it's a good list to get you started when you are trying to learn more about the importance of delivery, as well as about the myriad directions it can take.

- George Carlin
- Jerry Seinfeld
- Doug Stanhope
- Louis C.K.
- Doug Benson
- Ron White
- Maria Bamford
- Patton Oswalt
- Anthony Jeselnik
- Kathleen Madigan

Each of these comedians has a different and unique form of delivery for their brand of comedy. None is better than the other. They simply *work* for that particular comedian, and that's what is so important when it comes to humor.

Let's take it a step further and look at Kevin Smith's delivery. Smith, probably most well-known as a filmmaker and writer, also tours, records podcasts that are full of his brand of humor, and does his best to entertain his legions of fans. His delivery is much different from most others out there. While he is not a stand-up comedian by trade, he can certainly entrance and entertain an audience with his stories, most of which are very humorous.

Smith's delivery seems to derive very much from his personality. He's charming, self-deprecating, and has a wonderful way of weaving together stories that even many stand-ups don't have. Watching some of his specials or listening to his podcasts can be a great way to see just how his delivery differs and to see why it is effective for his style.

In fact, that's the real goal for anyone who tells a joke or tells a story – to come up with a unique delivery or style. Studying what has come before really helps in this regard.

Elements of Delivery
Let's also look at a list of some of the common elements found in the delivery of various comedians.

Raising your voice at the end of a sentence to add some punch

Waiting a beat before finishing a sentence

Changing the tempo of the story or joke to pull the crowd along with you

Using wild expressions and limb flailing – Dane Cook, we're looking at you

Bam, the double punch line

Props – yes, right about now, you should be thinking of the giant, buff Chucky doll that was once Carrot Top

These are just a few of the different delivery elements used by comedians. Once you start looking at more comics, you will start to recognize their special form of delivery as easily as you would the "tells" of everyone in your poker group.

The Importance of Timing in Comedy

Timing is everything in comedy. Or at least that's what everyone says. When you look at the best stand-up comedians who can really work a room and make people laugh, you can see it's true. If the timing is wrong, the set will fall flat. When you watch a comedic television show, you can start to feel the rhythm of the show after a while. If the timing is wrong, the show will feel wrong.

Timing really is everything, and it's not some magic "one-Mississippi, two-Mississippi" formula you can remember. Some people seem to be born with great comedic timing, while others have to work at it and develop it over time. It *is* possible for comedians to improve their timing.

One of the Most Vital Aspects of Comedy is...
Are you still waiting for it? Good, that's the point.

Keep waiting.

Keep waiting.

Anticipation is very important when it comes to comedy and *timing*. Comedians want to pull their audiences along with them, leading them like the Pied Piper until they are ready to deliver the final punch line. When a comedian can build that tension and hold it until the last possible minute, the comedic results are usually great.

Waiting too long, or not long enough, can be trouble, though! Again, it takes practice to make perfect. However, in some cases, *purposefully* misplaced timing can actually work quite well. This is not something that most comedians or comedy writers will generally want to try, though.

That's all. Move along now.

The Rule of Three
We will cover this in detail later in the book under the chapter on comedy writing. It is a good idea to understand the basics of what it is before we go further, though. The Rule of Three helps to build the tension and it can add the surprise or the twist.

You give an audience two similar things or two things they expect, and then the big change comes with number three. John Kinde's site HumorPower.com does a great job of illustrating just how the Rule of Three works.

Here are some of the patterns they illustrate on their site:

Extreme – Extreme – Ordinary

Ordinary – Ordinary – Extreme

Love – Love – Hate

Hate – Hate – Love

Expected –Expected – Unexpected

Category A – Category A – Category B

Can you guess what else makes liberal use of the Rule of Three? If you guessed horror, then give yourself a pat on the back. Once again, you can readily see the connection between these two genres.

Of course, once you know about the Rule of Three, you will start seeing it all the time. It can take away some of the surprise from horror, comedy, and more.

Yeah, But What About –

Are these the only things that are funny? Are these the only things that will make you laugh? Are you wondering about silly puppies, sneezing pandas, and grumpy cats? Aren't they funny? Well, they can be, and the endless fascination the population of the Internet has with these things, and the hits on viral videos and memes is proof of that. That sneezing baby panda and startled mom were hilarious, and it was all because of the anticipation, timing, and delivery.

So, yes, comedy can come from all over the place. If you think it's funny, it's probably funny. One of the reasons people find those animal videos funny is because they ascribe human traits and emotions to the animals in those videos.

When you start to examine just what it is that makes those things funny, you will generally find the humor comes from the *same rules as other humor*. The theories behind what makes those animal videos, or *Onion* news articles, *SNL* skits or anything else funny will be the same.

It's all in the execution, delivery, and timing of the piece. When you start to examine the things that make you laugh, you can see this.

Chapter 3:

What are the Different Types of Comedy?

As we continue the autopsy of comedy, it's important to know as many of the different types or styles of comedy possible. In this chapter, we will look at a number of these different comedy styles that you can find on stage, in writing, and on the screen.

It's important to keep in mind too that in many cases, comedic styles can cross over with one another. For example, parody and improv or sketch comedy can often go well together; see *Saturday Night Live* and *Chappelle's Show* as great examples of this. The point of this chapter is to look at all of the varying styles that are most popular today.

Parody
Parody has been around for quite a long time, and it is a very popular form of comedy. In fact, it all started in Greece when performers would create a poem or song that imitated the style of another poem or song. When you break down the word "parody," it actually comes from the Greek with "par" meaning beside, and "ody," or "ode," meaning song.

Parody eventually made its way toward modern society, and it is pervasive.

Modern Parody

Today, you can find parody just about everywhere. It's in songs, movies and television, and art. The parody is a type of satire, which we will learn more about later in this chapter. It makes fun of the original in some manner. People often like to see something they know, and perhaps love, turned on its head and made fun of a bit.

People view parody differently, though. Some see it as very funny, and even a form of flattery. Most people actually see it this way.

Others see it as ridicule and even mean-spirited. Devout fans of the original material can sometimes be very upset that someone had the audacity to make fun of something they love. The housewife and teen girl rage over the wealth of *Twilight* parodies was evidence of this!

Famous Examples of Parody

Parody Movies

Movies are probably the best-known form of parody out there today. It seems that new movies come out every year that parody the most popular films of the year before.

Here are some you are sure to know. If you haven't seen them, you might want to check them out so you can see how they parody the original. Just make sure you are familiar with the original materials so you can really understand what they are parodying. If you don't know the original, the parody will often seem pointless!

Spaceballs (parody of Star Wars)

Robin Hood: Men in Tights (parody of Robin Hood: Prince of Thieves as well as other Robin Hood films)

Blazing Saddles (Western parody)

History of the World (parody of the *actual* history of the world)

Hot Shots (parodies Top Gun, Rambo, etc.)

Young Frankenstein (parodies the story of Frankenstein as well as other monster movies)

Scary Movie (parodies a number of horror movies, including *Scream* in the first film)

Police Academy (parodies cop movies from the 1980s)

Austin Powers (parody of James Bond films)

Airplane! (surely you didn't think we'd forget this film that parodies the horde of disaster films from the 1970s)

You probably notice quite a bit of Mel Brooks populating this list. He's a master of comedy, especially when it comes to parody. You will also notice two horror parodies on this list. Once again, horror and comedy are twins.

Parody Music

Another area of parody that's quite popular is music. People have been parodying music since the time of the Greeks, and the comedic art form has been going strong ever since. Of course, when most people think of musical parody, the first name that comes to mind is Weird Al Yankovic.

He is one of the masters of musical parody, and he's been in the business of getting feet to tapping and mouths to laughing for decades now. Some of his most popular songs include:

"Eat It" (parodies Michael Jackson's "Beat It")

"Like a Surgeon" (parodies Madonna's "Like a Virgin")

"White and Nerdy" (parodies Chamillionaire's "Ridin'")

"Amish Paradise" (parodies "Gangsta's Paradise" from Coolio)

"The Saga Begins" (parodies "American Pie" and *Star Wars*)

Other Media

Magazines, such as *Mad Magazine* and *Cracked* parody movies and pop culture in general. Books, including *Bored of the Rings* (parodies *Lord of the Rings*) *Nightlight* (*Twilight* parody), and *Barry Trotter and the Unauthorized Parody* (Harry Potter, naturally) are popular methods of parody today as well.

The Internet has opened up all new possibilities. People are making their own songs, art, and movies that parody some of their favorite properties. If you want to see some examples of parody, just head to YouTube and start looking. You'll have hours, days, nay, a lifetime worth of stuff to watch. Of course, the quality varies.

Oh, the Legal Horrors of Parody
The only thing as popular as parody is suing over parody. Many of the original rights holders who have their materials parodied are not happy about it. They feel as though the parody might hurt their original property, and they do the first thing that comes to mind – SUE.

Many lawsuits hit the court systems each year, and most of the time, the courts find in the favor of the people who are doing the parodying. Parody is perfectly legal according to the law. That doesn't stop people from filing lawsuits though.

Satire

Some people may think that parody and satire are the same thing, but that's not true. The goal of satire is generally a bit different. With parody, people are mostly looking to have some fun. Satire can be fun, and it generally is. However, even though it may be comical, it often exposes real issues and problems. It can focus on an individual, a community, country, or the world.

They are quite closely related, but there are enough differences that you should try to keep them separate in your mind.

Satire does not have to focus on political events or personalities, but it often does. It can also cover celebrities, sports, and everyday events.

In order to get a better idea of what qualifies as satire, it is a good idea to look at some of the best modern examples.

The Daily Show

The Colbert Report

Saturday Night Live Weekend Update

Satire in the comics – Political comics in particular

Satire in literature – Works from Mark Twain are great examples

Some of the other types of satire, which we will dive into deeper a bit later, include irony and sarcasm. As we mentioned, different types of comedy often blur the lines and cross into one another. That can certainly happen with satire.

Before we go, here's a list of some of the best satirists. To learn more about this branch of comedy, and tragedy really, you can check out the work from these folks.

- George Orwell
- Ambrose Bierce
- Jonathan Swift
- Plato
- Bob Odenkirk
- Trey Parker and Matt Stone

That's right, you just got a list that has both the guys from *South Park* and Plato. Yeah, Plato is good enough to be next to Parker and Stone.

Slapstick

From the bit of satire to the physical pain of slapstick, here's another genre of comedy that has been popular for a long time. As a matter of fact, the first comedian was probably some caveman named Nub who realized that if he slipped and fell, the other cave folk would hoot, howl, and laugh. He was the first ham. Thus came the birth of slapstick.

Of course, that's probably not how things happened at all, but it's nice to imagine that they might have! Real slapstick has a more definitive origin, though, at least when it comes to what we consider this form of modern comedy.

The Origins of Slapstick

Slapstick comedy was popular in cinema almost from the get go. Some of the earliest performers on film were slapstick legends. According to the Comedy Knockout website, Ben Turpin was the first to be hit in the face with a pie. Mabel Normand was the first real "woman of slapstick." Famous faces such as Buster Keaton and Charlie Chaplin soon followed suit with their own unique brand of slapstick comedy.

The origins of slapstick come from people that we today consider true legends of Hollywood. So, it can't be all that bad.

Is Slapstick Legit Comedy?

While there are certainly different schools of thought when it comes to the legitimacy or value of slapstick, most people can't deny that it's funny at its core. Little kids love watching slapstick, and the highbrow adults who think it is just another form of low humor might actually be missing the point.

You do not have to be an erudite snob about your comedy. Go back to the very basics of humor. If you laugh, then it's funny. After all, isn't comedy *supposed* to make you feel joy and laugh? When you take too much of this pure silly joy from comedy, it can be dry and actually boring in some cases.

Do you know what that means?

It means that sometimes – not all the time, but *sometimes* – a guy getting hit in the privates or slipping on a banana peel is just darned funny. You laughed at it when you were a kid, and it's okay to laugh at it now, even though your hipster friends might not agree.

If slapstick humor did not have a place today, why do the *Jackass* films and others like them do so well? Slapstick has its place, and most feel that slapstick is a classic element of many comedies today.

Come and Knock on Our Door

For example, think about the show *Three's Company*. Much of the humor in that show comes from misunderstanding, the unexpected, and the slapstick style of the charming and unbreakable John Ritter.

Watch Out for the Ottoman!

Another example of slapstick on television is the classic *The Dick Van Dyke Show*. Dick Van Dyke had a lanky body and a way of tripping, slipping, oozing, and falling through certain scenes that made it look as though he was one of the most klutzy people on the planet. He did it in a way that looked natural and could get audiences howling and laughing. Of course, he was also a dancer, so he was able to do everything gracefully and easily – he just looked like a klutz!

You Know the Theme Song, so Start Humming in 4,3,2...

Another great comedian who utilized slapstick in many of his routines was Benny Hill. *The Benny Hill Show* was a British program known the world over. The show's star made liberal use of parody, mime, double-entendre, and, of course, slapstick.

It's one of the strangest and funniest shows to air. It had some similarities to the Keystone Kops, but Hill's themes generally tended to run a bit more toward the raunchy side.

Where is Slapstick Today?

Today, there just isn't the same wealth of slapstick as there once was, at least when it comes to adult comedy. It's still there, but it does not have the same power and widespread usage as it once did. That's not to say it isn't still funny, but audiences tend to cycle through things that they find hilarious.

It's not dead though. It is too durable and timeless to ever actually go away from comedy completely. Every time your friend stumbles or drops something, every time you upend a plate of spaghetti onto the rug, you are taking part in your very own slapstick routine. When that happens, you have to deal with the tragedy of a messy carpet... and to continue beating a dead horse, those duplicitous siblings of comedy and tragedy unite once again.

You never have to worry about slapstick in mainstream media,

either. There's a good chance that slapstick will one day return with a vengeance... a tripping, falling, bumbling vengeance.

Sarcasm

Sarcasm as a form of humor has a bit of debate surrounding it that won't go away. In fact, the debate has been there since around the time Oscar Wilde said that sarcasm was the "lowest form of wit."

Others consider it the highest form of wit. And the argument continues.

Most of those who consider it a high form of wit happen to be sarcastic, though, so it can be hard to tell if they are serious and egotistical or if they are being sarcastic about the entire thing… and then the logic of their argument, and the question of their intelligence, just starts circling the drain.

Most people feel that sarcasm is a legit form of humor, but it can be overused and it can be used simply to spew bile at others. If the sarcastic person is sarcastic simply to hurt or put down others without a legitimate reason to be sarcastic, other than the fact that they can, it's not comedy. It's just being a jerk.

Sarcasm is one of those forms of humor that most people, and comedians (yes, they are people too), have to tread carefully. You can go from being funny and sarcastic to being on the end of a heaping dose of intense Twitter hate in a matter of minutes.

So What Is Sarcasm?
While Wilde might have considered it low wit, a master of sarcasm needs to have a quick wit no matter how high off the ground it might be. Sarcasm requires rapid-fire remarks and jokes in an effort to hurt someone else or to deride a situation or a statement the person made. The tone of voice is important as well, and it can convey a number of different things.

Sarcasm can be about nearly anything, but the goal is to hurt the other party or to silence them. It's easy to see how this can be construed as mean because, well, it really is at its heart.

Still, some people develop their sense of sarcasm as a defense or coping mechanism. They may not always realize just how much their words really damage other people. Then again, there are some sarcastic sociopaths out there that know exactly what they are doing.

Sarcastic All-Stars

If you want to get a better understanding of sarcasm out in the wilds of comedy, it's a good idea to look at some of the individuals that tend to be quite good at it. Here's a quick list of some of the comedians who embrace their sarcastic powers and use them for good and for evil.

Bill Murray – The guy is so good that he can deliver sarcasm without you even realizing you've just been on the receiving end of it.

David Cross – The brilliant comedian, possibly best known as Tobias on *Arrested Development*, is a master of irony, sarcasm, and having a smart mouth.

Daniel Tosh – Tosh is another guy who has sarcasm mastered. Like Murray, he can be sarcastic right to someone's face without them getting upset, and sometimes without them realizing what happened. He's able to do this with charm and an upbeat personality.

Sarah Silverman – Attractive and hilarious, Silverman's style contains a healthy amount of sarcasm. She's a great comedian to study if you want to know more about sarcasm.

Sarcasm might not be for everyone, and it can be very difficult to convey in writing. In fact, some arguments on the Internet start because people don't know when others are being sarcastic and when they are being genuine. They often get angry at one another for no real reason, and that's an entire different realm of funny right there.

Farce

A farce is a type of comedy that has a basis in coincidences that are entirely too impossible for the real world, and most works of farce will also have quite a bit of satire in them. They have many elements in them that are too outrageous or ridiculous to be true. As the comedy continues, things get wilder and wilder, and they become even more ridiculous.

Some great examples of farce in movies include the following films. Keep in mind that many of these films use other techniques, in addition to being farcical, that help them to achieve their overall comedic effect.

There's Something About Mary

The 40-Year-Old Virgin

Anchorman

Duck Soup (and much of the work from the Marx Brothers, for that matter)

The Hangover

National Lampoon's Vacation

Spies Like Us

Blind Date

Ace Ventura: Pet Detective

Tropic Thunder

This is just a small sample of all of the fun farcical films out there

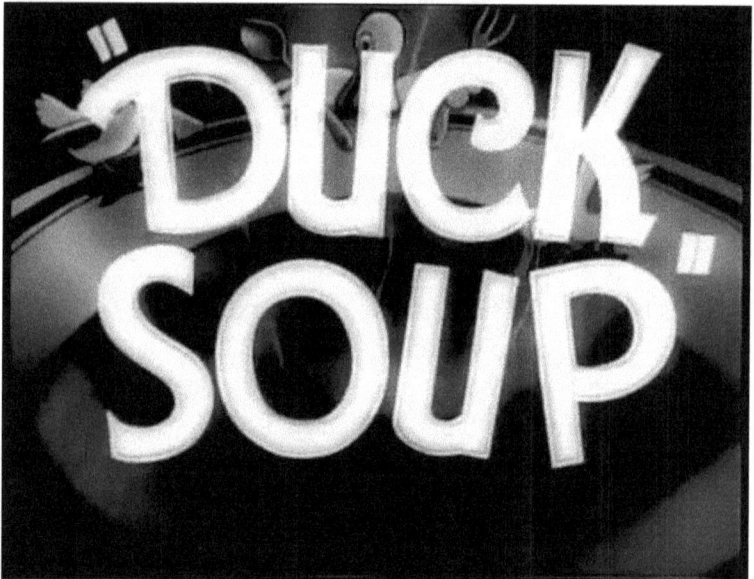

today. If you like these sorts of films, you have quite a long list from which you can choose.

Surreal

Surrealism has been a part of literature for ages, but it's a relatively recent transplant to comedy. It was after WWII that surreal comedy really started to take hold. Shows on radio and then on television would feature purposefully ridiculous and strange plots and characters, which helped to boost the comedy effect.

Surrealism soon became an alternate form of comedy that was certainly not in the mainstream. The television shows and the stand-up comedians who embraced it liked it that way. They had their audience and the audience for fringe humor is such that it would often be very loyal.

A great example of a comedy show that strayed into the realm of the surreal as well as the farcical quite often was *Monty Python's Flying Circus*.

Part of surrealism was about defying expectations. You feel you understand the world, and the joke the comedian is about to tell, and then he or she takes it in a direction that you just didn't expect. Yes, that's really the essence of comedy in general, but surrealists would take it to a different level.

One very good example is Steve Coogan. He would start jokes that began down a path that the audience was sure would lead to something sexist or even racist, but the punch line of the joke would be something politically correct. This really defied what the audience thought would happen, and it would often make those audience members question themselves. If they were *so sure* he was going to have a racist or sexist punch line, what did it say about them and their expectations in the world?

Surrealist comedy at its best – and all comedy, actually – can do more than make you laugh. It can also make you think. Yet again, *South Park* is very good at that. If you are looking for a stand-up comedian who is one of the best surrealist comedians, look no further than Steven Wright. His deadpan delivery of odd humor is one of the best examples out there.

Black Comedy

Another term for this is gallows humor. While a substantial amount of comedy uses tragedy, as we've discussed, this takes things to an entirely different level. Dark comedy uses humor to make light of very serious situations. It has been a part of literature, television, and movies for a long time.

Even though it is not mainstream entertainment by any stretch of the imagination, devotees find the subject matter and style of humor their favorite. Freud actually wrote an essay on the subject and how it can help people to cope with hopeless and dangerous situations. At its essence, it is about being funny even in the worst and most horrific of situations.

Many people in the military, law enforcement, and in the medical field adopt this type of humor. Again, they do this not because they are heartless or cruel, but so they can cope with the reality of what is happening around them.

In some cases, the humor can also take on something of a surreal tone, although this is not always the case. Sometimes, the actual horror is just as important as the comedy, and they do not want to dampen that with surrealism.

Some Good Examples of Dark Comedy

Naturally, many horror comedies will fall into this category. So do quite a few television shows. *M*A*S*H* is a perfect example of this. They treated the war and the horrors of war as a black comedy. Let's look at some of the other examples of dark humor.

Death at a Funeral

Thank You for Smoking

Shaun of the Dead

Rubber

Heathers

Raising Arizona

American Psycho

The Royal Tenenbaums

Very Bad Things

Dr. Strangelove

Of course, dark comedy goes beyond the screen. It's a huge part of the stage as well, and you can find quite a few comedians famous for their dark brand of humor. Here are a few you might want to consider checking out when you are in the mood for something bleak and funny.

- Russell Brand
- Richard Pryor
- Bill Hicks
- Lenny Bruce
- Chris Morris
- Bill Burr

Improv

Improv happens on a stage, but it's not stand-up comedy – not by a long shot. However, there is often quite a bit of crossover. Many comedians are also improvisational specialists, which is what helps them to be fast with their wits and their words when need be. Many who haven't actually seen an improv show actually don't know what to expect, and it's natural that they think it's something similar to stand-up. It's important that we make the distinction, though.

The Gist of Improv

Improv has one person or a group of people who are working together and making up the story of what is happening as they go along. They are technically writing the story as it unfolds, and this is not an easy feat.

Many improv shows will start with a suggestion from the audience. For example, the group might request a setting from the audience, and someone in the crowd might blurt out "doctor's office" or "carnival." It doesn't have to be a location the group asks for, either. They might ask for a profession, and someone from the crowd could call out "snake charmer" or "goalie for the Red Wings."

The goal of the group members is then to create a sketch that focuses on whatever the suggestion might be. The kicker is that they don't have any time to confer on what the sketch should be. They just have to do it right then and there.

The group doesn't just throw anything into their act, though. They take the suggestions and use their skills to create actual stories for the sketches so they can add the necessary structure to each of the scenes. If they don't have the skills to do this, things become chaotic rather quickly.

People have to know and study improv in order to become good at it. They need to work and practice with others in the group so they can develop their skills. Fortunately, there are some rules that can help with this process.

The following rules of improv, developed from an article by David Alger, are a part of just about every group out there today:

Say "Yes, and"

Add new information for the scene

Don't block the progression of the other actors

Don't ask questions unless you also add information to the scene

Change the direction

Focus on the scene and the lines happening at the moment rather than what you will say next – you need to make sure you are following the flow of the scene rather than doing your own thing

Provide details the others can use

Establish the location

Focus on the right thing based on the type of scene you are developing whether it is the character, the situation, or the objects in the scene

Everything should serve the scene and its progression

It takes quite a bit of practice, and time to get comfortable with a group, before an improv group can really perform well together. Of course, performers who have been doing it for years can often come into a scene with a new group without any issues.

If you want to see some great ways of *not* doing improv, you should check out season 2, episode 9 of the American version of *The Office*. Steve Carrell's character Michael Scott goes to his improv class, which is none to happy to see him, and subsequently ruins it.

Famous Improv Groups
Many stars get their start in improv groups. It is a great way to improve many different comedic skills in addition to improvisation. It helps with timing, for example. Some of the most famous stars working today with backgrounds in improv include Tina Fey, Amy Poehler, and Bill Murray.

Groups you might know include:

Second City in Chicago

Upright Citizens Brigade in NYC

Improv Asylum in Boston

Loose Moose Theatre in Calgary, Alberta, Canada

Groundlings in Los Angeles

Improv Television – It's a Thing

Improv is popular in the clubs, but it has made its way to television as well. Two of the shows include *Drew Carey's Improv-A-Ganza* and *Whose Line is It Anyway?*, both of which are very popular today.

Some shows that might seem as though they have a full script are actually heavily improvised. The scripts for *Reno 911!* are a good example. While the scripts had a general direction and usually a main storyline on which the actors could focus, quite a bit of the show was improvised on the spot. This lent a very different feel to this popular and beloved show that it wouldn't have had if it went strictly by a script.

Anecdotal

Here's a definition of comedy style that's short and sweet. It also happens to be one of the most used styles of comedy. In fact, just about everyone, even those who aren't comedians, uses it. Anecdotal comedy is story-based. The comedian or writer tells a story based on something that happened to them in real life.

However, they add a few embellishments and funny bits to turn a regular story that might elicit a smile or a chuckle into a story that will really bring the laughter. Many comedians make use of this type of comedy. In fact, most comedians make use of this technique today. It helps to connect them with their audience, and it is quite a bit more entertaining than the rapid-fire jokes spit out of the mouths of comedians of a bygone era.

Of course, there is always an exception to the rule. Steven Wright's style of humor lends itself well to the rapid-fire approach rather than the long stories.

His deadpanning and matter-of-fact attitude with his delivery, no matter how surreal the subject might be, works well, especially with that rapid approach. The audience is just catching up and he's already on to the next joke. This makes his sets seem to go quickly.

How True Do the Anecdotes Have to Be?
Just how honest are all those comedians up on stage? While most of the stories they tell likely have some basis in fact, truth and humor don't always travel the same path. Sometimes, in order to make something funny, the comedian, writer, or even you, has to do a bit of historical revision to make the story fit the beats and patterns you need to make it truly funny.

Is it lying? In the most basic sense, it is, but then so is all storytelling. If you are exaggerating to get a few laughs, or you do it for a living on stage, exaggeration and even lies aren't a big deal. Of course, if you are trying to pass things off as biographical and real, then you had better not lie!

Blue
What is blue comedy? It doesn't have anything to do with the Blue Man Group, that's for sure. It doesn't even have to be "blue collar" humor. Blue comedy is off-color and it can be on the dirty side. It might use language and cover topics that you might not talk about in "polite company." The typical types of jokes might include sexual situations and rough jokes that sailors, construction workers, and the rest of the Village People might appreciate.

Actually, many people like to listen to this type of humor because it can seem a bit naughty, and it is generally quite funny. Who are some of the biggest and best comedians to engage in this type of humor? Some on the following list are obvious and others might surprise you.

Sarah Silverman – She's a comedian that utilizes many types of comic elements in her humor, including sarcasm and blue humor. She pushes the limits of good taste whether she is on a television show, such as *The Sarah Silverman Program* or she's doing stand-up.

Dave Attell – He's another comedian that goes further than most with race jokes and sexual situations in his humor. His humor, while funny, can actually make some people cringe a bit!

Bob Saget – *Full House* from the late '80s was a saccharine-soaked dose of family-friendly humor starring Bob Saget as the ultra good-guy dad Danny Tanner, who hearkened back to the days of black-and-white sitcom dads who were bumbling and overly sweet. His stand-up comedy is the exact opposite. The man's jokes are outrageous and downright funny, though, and he's one of the better comedians working today. Looking back, the sweet work Saget did on *Full House* might just be the best bit of acting television has ever seen!

Deadpan

Deadpan can be a difficult comic technique to incorporate, and it is not for everyone. Some people are great at deadpan comedy, and they can tell their jokes or come off sarcastic without a change in their facial expression or body language.

Doing this and still eliciting a response from the audience is not easy to do, though, and that's why it is not something all comedians use.

Some comedians see this technique as a huge part of their delivery style, and it can come to define them over the years. Others see deadpanning as something they can use occasionally. They keep it as just another tool in their toolbox.

A Different Delivery

To make deadpan humor work, it is extremely important to have a good setup for the joke. Since the comedian is speaking in monotone for this type of comedy, the actual delivery tone isn't going to change. It is a steady method of delivery, and if you don't have the setup perfected, the joke can fall flat, or it can go over the heads of those listening to it simply because you are deadpanning and they don't hear a change in your voice's cadence, which is a trick other comedians use.

When a comedian gets it right though, it can set the room ablaze with laughter. The key is for the comedian to continue with the deadpan without breaking and laughing. Some of the best comedians who utilize deadpanning include:

- Jim Gaffigan
- Mike Birbiglia
- Demetri Martin
- Steven Wright
- Mitch Hedburg

In addition to the comedians mentioned here, entire television shows make use of this sort of deadpanning for the delivery of many of their funniest moments. *The Office* (both the U.S. and U.K. versions) and *Parks & Recreation* are two great examples that make quite a bit of use of deadpanning. They are very successful at it too.

Keep an eye out for other uses of deadpanning in television shows. You will find that it is used more than you might imagine. Dry British humor is famous for this.

Just the Beginning

Comedians and writers have hundreds of different types and styles of humor and comedic elements they can use. Consider puns and wordplay, the use of misunderstanding, double-entendre, and more. All of these different methods are valid forms of humor. Some you will find funnier than you do others.

In the following chapter, we will examine some of the reasons some people think some things are funny and they don't think other things are funny. It's actually a bit more complex than simply taste.

As you start to watch more stand-up comics, and you start to watch more movies and television shows with comedic elements, you will see how all of these elements in this chapter, in addition to other elements, come together as a basis for so much of the comedy we see today. The best way to learn about comedy is by studying it and watching it.

Chapter 4

Why Do Different People Find Different Things Funny?

In this chapter, we'll look at why you might find something funny, but someone else you know might not find it funny. It can get a bit tricky, and it can encompass a number of different things. We'll try to keep things as simple and as straightforward as possible.

Some people might say that they simply don't get it. Others might say it's offensive. Still others might simply look at you through their monocle and mutter something like "lowbrow." Others might not be able to explain why they don't find something funny.

However, it really tends to boil down to the items in this chapter. Let's start deconstructing the funny and the not-so-funny to see what it is that makes people laugh or stay icily silent.

Experience Required

One of the first things that you have to consider is whether the person listening to the joke or seeing the movie has any experience with the situation the comedy entails. For example, if you are telling an airplane joke to a person who has no idea what an airplane is, the joke won't go over very well. When you have to over-explain something, it strips it of its humor.

Some jokes may be universal, but *not all of them are*. You might not understand certain jokes or elements of humor that people in the middle of the Gobi Desert find funny. They probably wouldn't know how to respond to your humorous story about running out of toilet paper while at Chili's, either.

The difference in experience doesn't necessarily have to be because someone is from another country, either. People from various geographic locations in the United States have different experiences too. So do people with differing social and economic statuses.

The show *30 Rock* did a great send up of this. Tracy Morgan's character is having trouble with his stand-up routine, and he can't figure out why. The show flashbacks to his original material, which was for the common man, and they show what he's doing now – material about the troubles of dining on lobster and not being able to close the roof of his mansion.

Comedians who want to go over well need to make sure they know their audience and what they expect. They have to connect with common types of experiences.

Culture Club

This goes along with experience quite nicely. People from different cultures grow up with different ideas of what comedy is and isn't.

For example, the over-the-top, in-your-face style humor that is so popular in the United States is not nearly as popular in Britain. You would think that the two nations have quite a bit in common, so humor should be a commonality as well, but you would be dead wrong. They have a different sensibility based on their culture. Some call it refined, some call it stuffy. Regardless, the difference in the cultures really can make something appear unfunny because it *is* unfunny to that particular audience.

It's this way with every culture. They will find some things funny and others not funny. This is one of the reasons that when television shows receive a remake in another country, they can't just take the scripts word for word and expect the same success. They need to inject a bit of their own culture into those scripts in order for them to play well at home.

The S-Word

Okay, for starters, you can pick your mind up out of the gutter. It's not Bob Saget talking here and it's not *that* S-word that we're talking about. We're talking about another word you should be quite familiar with by this point in the book – *subjectivity*. Yes, sweet dead horse, humor is subjective, and sometimes the answer really is as simple as that. Some things make some people laugh and they don't make other people. It's the way it is, and you can't spend too much time beating yourself up about it.

Oh, the Peer Pressure

Peer pressure can do some strange things. You might feel as though you *want* to laugh at something that happens or something that you watch on television, but you might not laugh if you see that none of your friends or family or coworkers are laughing.

Humans are silly creatures that often allow others to dictate what we find appealing or funny. If you are around a group of people that don't feel slapstick is funny, chances are you won't laugh at that type of humor either.

In this case and others like it, the group collective can override people's individual tastes. Sometimes, it's just easier from a group standpoint to keep your laughter inside if you find something to be uproariously funny and no one else laughs. If you burst out laughing at what others may feel is an inappropriate time, you can be sure you will get some stares and people will question your sense of humor.

Keep in mind that your sense of humor *is not wrong*. Whatever it was, you found it funny and it worked for you. Still, it is important to make sure that you are using your best judgment on when and where to let the world know that you find nothing funnier than unexpected and loud bodily functions.

For example, if you are in a room with your boss and other managers at your company, it might be in your best interest to follow suit on what is and is not funny – at *least* until you get home and tell your friends what happened after your boss ate chili for lunch.

How Old Are You Now?
When we are little, we find some very odd things to be quite funny. Clowns, strange cartoons that don't make a lick of sense to anyone over the age of four, clapping, dust motes, peek-a-boo, and similar things. The things that we find funny will often change and grow along with people as they age and learn more about the world.

Little children will laugh at different sorts of things than teens will, and many teenagers find things funny that simply go over the heads of the adults. Adults will laugh at things the kids don't laugh at. It's all about age, experience, and maturity.

Granted, we all have those things in different amounts, and that's why so many things can seem funny to so many different people and why other things can fall flat. Many writers and filmmakers today understand this, and they take pains to make sure the material they are creating for kids will appeal to both young and old alike.

Consider films such as *Shrek, Toy Story, Up,* and others. They have stories and gags that a wide audience will get and will find funny. Movies from the past, such as *A Christmas Story,* could do this as well. Another good one, which happens to deal with Christmas as well, is *Elf,* starring Will Ferrell

Still, some people don't find those films funny. They find all of the humor to be juvenile and feel they are too sophisticated for it. That might be true. It might also mean that one or more of the *other* reasons we're looking at in this chapter are coming into play in that person's life.

Closeness to the Tragedy of the Subject

This one is actually one of the most common reasons as to why people might not find something funny. Even those people who feel that humor should be open and that everything should be fair game generally have at least one subject that they find taboo or off limits.

Jokes exist about absolutely everything today, including murder, natural disasters, terror attacks, assaults, and every other atrocity that you can imagine. Whether this is good or bad, or funny or unfunny, depends on whom you are.

Some people can see humor as a way to cope with and understand those terrible things. They seek out the humor as much as they can because they feel the world would be too dark a place without it.

For those folks, the jokes about the morbid are still funny despite the pain from which they stem. In fact, it might be able to provide them with some catharsis to help them get over residual pain.

However, sometimes, even those people who have suffered from cancer, who have had relatives die, or who have been the victim of a crime can look at some of the jokes that touch upon those things and laugh. It generally takes a lot of time before they can find those things humorous, but many will eventually reach that spot.

Again, tragedy with the right amount of time equals humor. Yet, that's not always the case. Some people will never find a joke about AIDS funny, just as they won't find jokes about the Holocaust or 9/11 funny.

Execution of the Funny

Another possibility is that the joke's execution, the delivery of the joke and the punch line, or the style of comedy someone is attempting simply falls flat. Some might laugh to be polite, but the joke itself might just not be that good. If you don't laugh in those cases, don't feel too bad about it. In fact, if others are laughing at something and you don't laugh, never feel bad about it. It is all... subjective.

The Gender Gap

Sometimes, things that men might find funny are repugnant to women. Some of the things that women will find funny will go right over the heads of many men. Our gender can affect what we find funny and even how we process different sorts of humor.

Of course, it's not as though men and women never find the same things funny. It's just that gender really can play a role in humor. Think back to your days on the playground as a child. Boys might think that chasing girls with bugs they find is a great laugh, but the girls likely have a very different take on that!

It's not only humor, either. Look at many of the things that men and women find fun, and you will find quite a bit of disparity in many cases. There is crossover, naturally, but you can't deny that gender plays a definite role.

Can Laughter Ever Be Bad?

Thus far, we've talked about all of the great things about laughter. It has some health benefits, it makes you feel great, and it can bring people together. However, there really can be a dark side to humor.

If the things that make people laugh are at the total expense of others, or because others are in actual emotional or physical pain, it's not funny. It means something is desperately wrong with the people who are causing that pain.

In the End

What it all comes down to is a combination of the above factors. Who you are, where you grow up, whom you associate with, and what has happened to you in your life all affect the things that you will or will not find funny. If you find something funny, good. If someone else doesn't, it's no big deal.

One More Theory

Of course, there is always the slight possibility that the subject who isn't laughing is actually an unfeeling robot, such as Data from *Star Trek* or Megatron from the movies where Michael Bay blows things up. Not that movie. No, the other one. No, not that one either. The one where he has explosions. That's right, the one where things go boom. There you go, now you get it.

Granted, this is a stretch. Chances are there aren't robots running around and frowning at everything you find funny. You can never be too cautious with robots, though.

And there was an example of something a bit farcical!

Chapter 5

The Science of Funny

It's time to don our lab coats, wild hair, and latex gloves. Grab the beakers and other science things and let's dissect comedy to see what's so funny! Of course, it's not that simple. In fact, the more we learn about the brain and the more we learn about laughter, the less we really know.

People have been thinking about comedy and laughter for millennia. Plato and Aristotle both spent time trying to figure out what it was about humans that made us want to laugh so much. They wondered why humor was so important to happiness, and we still aren't entirely sure of the reasons today.

Who and What Laughs?

Who and what can laugh and giggle? Isn't it just us humans? Well, according to research, that's not the case. Other primates, including gorillas, chimps, and orangutans have their own form of laughter. That doesn't mean that somewhere deep in the Congo is a stand-up comedy club populated by gorillas. It does mean that laughter – and the anticipation of laughter – is present in creatures besides humans.

One of the reasons researchers know this is because when a baby primate is tickled, it does the primate version of laughing. When someone *pretends* to tickle the baby, it does the *same thing* because it anticipates being tickled.

Why Do They Laugh?

Why does this happen? Different theories abound.

Some believe that it is evolutionary in all primates, and that it might even be in some other animals as well. Some feel it was a response to danger. The primates would laugh when the danger was not as great as they thought it was at first, and they used the laughter as a way to tell other primates, "Hey, don't worry."

Others feel that the reason laughter is important in all primates is to teach the young to get along with one another. They view laughter as a social tool that developed in primates, and that actually does make sense. As humans evolved, our idea of humor evolved along with it. We embraced humor so much that we've created industries devoted entirely to making us laugh.

The real reason is that we just don't know, and chances are that we will probably never know. Unless Professor Banana Pants of Chimps University comes out and explains it to us silly humans, it's likely to be a long road paved with more research and opposing theories.

In the chapters that follow, we'll get deeper into the different philosophical theories of comedy. For now though, we'll continue down this scientific path to see what we might be able to find.

How Often Do We Laugh?

How much do we like to laugh? According to the University of Western Ontario, a professor (not Professor Banana Pants, by the way), calculated just how much the average person laughs each day. Research showed that we laugh about 17.5 times a day. The half a laugh may come from old episodes of *Mr. Belvedere* or *ALF*, we're not entirely sure.

What's Happening in that Brain of Yours?

So, what is it that makes us laugh? As you should know by now, it could be just about anything that tickles our funny bone. Thanks to modern medical technology though, we can now actually see just how the brain works and what it does when it finds something to be funny.

Let's look at how they can do this. Beware: it gets a bit... *sciencey.*

Okay, How *Do* They Do This?
Functional magnetic resonance imaging is the key to looking into the brain to see how it responds to different stimulus. Dartmouth scientists hooked subjects up to these machines and had them watch episodes of *Seinfeld* and *The Simpsons*. They would then observe what happened to the peoples' brains as they watched the shows.

Here's where it gets interesting. Even though the subjects might not always laugh aloud at the happenings on the screen, their brain still reacted. The researchers were able to see changes in the brain as people started to see the setup to the joke, and another change when the joke landed.

They noticed that the detection of the joke would occur in the "left frontal and posterior temporal cortices on the left side of the brain." When you stop to think about it, that's quite impressive. Keep this in mind (see what we did there?) in the following chapters, particularly the one on incongruity theory that talks about contradictions in situations and unexpected results.

The scans and the theory tie in nicely together, and it means there could be something to all of these different comedy theories after all.

Deeper into the Realm of Science
Other experiments that utilized the same equipment found that certain types of comedy – pratfalls and verbal jokes – needed a person's brain to have basic language-processing skills in order to work as humor. This equates, at a basic level, to people needing to have certain experiences in life in order to appreciate different sorts of humor.

Understanding language is very important, as it helps people put together words and scenarios that might be incongruous at first and only make sense when one dissects the punch line. Those who have the language skills can decipher the punch line in less than a second most of the time, which is why laughter at those types of jokes is generally instantaneous. Of course, a few people always look around at everyone and say, "I don't get it."

Those who have lesser language skills may have some trouble with understanding and appreciating puns, for example. Kids who don't know as many words and who do not have the same experience as adults don't always get puns. When they do though, kids tend to like them because it is a simple form of humor and is one they can remember and repeat.

They often do repeat their puns too, along with their other jokes. They subject anyone who is in the vicinity – parents, siblings, teachers... they are all in danger from little kid jokes that *require* laughter from the adults in question, lest the child question your taste in humor.

Well, That's a Punch in the Face

Another study shows that people who had damage to their frontal lobe would have more trouble understanding punch lines. This means that those individuals preferred other types of humor, with slapstick being the most popular because it is easier to follow and understand.

Does this mean that everyone who enjoys slapstick humor has brain damage? No, of course it doesn't! Remember the subjectivity of humor. People like what they like. It's just that some people may have an easier time processing certain things as funny, and that's the reason they lean toward a particular type of comedy.

Why the Joy and Laughter, Though?

We can now see the basic brain processes as it sees and acknowledges that something is funny. However, we also want to know just what it is that makes us happy when this happens. Well, it's actually quite simple. The brain will give us a little treat when we find something funny.

It releases dopamine, which we perceive as pleasure. That's why laughing feels so good. When people are feeling upset or they are having a bout of depression, it can be difficult to laugh, and this is because the brain just doesn't give us that dopamine.

The Magic Joke, the Ultimate Laugh, and the Perfect Humorous Algorithm

If we can see when the brain fires up and says, "Hey, that's funny," and we can record and understand those patterns, it might seem as though there should be some type of formula for creating perfect jokes that work all the time and that work on everyone. Comedians and writers around the world would probably do anything to get their hands on such a formula, too.

Of course, it doesn't exist.

Why doesn't it exist? You should be used to what's happening by now. You already know the word that comes next. That's right; there *can't* be a formula for the perfect joke because humor is subjective.

In addition to the subjectivity, one also has to consider the context. Laughing with friends is much different from laughing with total strangers.

As we mentioned in the last chapter, the relationship you have with the subject of the comedy is important in determining whether you will or will not laugh. All of those things from the last chapter play a role here and they throw a wrench in your devilish plans to come up with the ultimate joke.

You can't do it.

That doesn't stop people from trying though, and that is a very good thing. It means that comedy will keep on growing and changing and people will always be looking for ways to come up with the best material possible. This is great for comedy lovers everywhere, even if they don't all happen to laugh at the same thing.

What the What?

Here's a head-scratcher for you. Even though we've seen into the brain so we know when people are understanding jokes and then laughing at them, researchers also found out something else. Psychologists observed that sometimes, quite often actually, people laughed even when there was no joke or no actual real stimulus that one would think should elicit laughter.

What they discovered was the friendliness, playfulness, being in a group setting, and being in a positive atmosphere were all great ways to make people laugh. You didn't even have to say anything particularly clever. People felt comfortable with one another and they were in the mood to be jovial. That led to smiles and laughter and elevated levels of dopamine, which led to more pleasure and more laughter.

So, laughter is possible even without any actual comedy or any funny things happening. Thanks so much for clearing that up, science.

Chapter 6

The Superiority Theory

Plato and Aristotle, two of the earliest philosophers to try to understand humor, were big proponents of this theory. When you learn what the Superiority Theory is, you might conclude that these guys were either jerks or they had little faith in humanity. Chances are it was the latter.

What is the Superiority Theory?

This theory proposes that comedy stems from the misfortune or the lower position of others. People laugh at the bad things that happen to other people. They may laugh because they can relate to the situation or because they feel fortunate that they are not in that situation.

Plato was so adamant that this theory was true that he felt that any humor in stories about the gods should be removed when told to children. He felt that if they did not remove the humor, the kids would feel superior and then would lose their respect for the gods.

Thomas Hobbes, another philosopher, came to a similar conclusion in the 1800s. In his essay "Human Nature," he said that "the passion of laughter is nothing else but sudden glory arising from some sudden conception of some eminency in ourselves, by comparison with the infirmity of others, or with our own formerly."

This simply means that when something bad or misfortunate happens to someone else, we laugh and take great delight in it. Of course, that's lowbrow, right? You would never dream of laughing at something so pedestrian and mundane. Or would you?

The Superiority Theory in Action

Let's look at a good and simple example of this type of theory in action. Let's say that you and your friend are walking along a hilltop on a beautiful winter afternoon. As you reach the crest of the hill, your friend bends down to pick something up and the seam on the rear of his pants rips. He stands up suddenly, loses his balance, falls, and then careens down the hill faster than a little kid on a sled would before finally spinning to a stop at the bottom.

Are you not going to laugh at that? Most people out there will. The rest can look down on us with their moral superiority and that's fine, but most people will laugh in that situation.

That's the essence of the Superiority Theory: People laughing at the expense of other people. Is this a good thing, though?

Negative Factors of the Superiority Theory

Do people laugh at this type of humor? We've already established that they do, and that you may even be one of those people who laugh at other peoples' expense on occasion.

However, no one likes to be the one on the receiving end of this. Put yourself in that situation. In fact, most people don't have to think very hard about this because they have been in that situation before – and likely will be again. Being the butt of the joke isn't fun. You would not want to be the one at the bottom of that snowy hill, and you wouldn't want friends, family, and even strangers to point and laugh at you.

Yet, we seem to have a disconnection when those bad things happen to someone else. Even as adults, if someone drops a plate of food or their drink at a buffet, there's still that laughter and even applause that you would expect from a cafeteria in a middle school rather than a restaurant.

Since experience is a part of what makes humor subjective, perhaps some people laugh when this happens because they remember being in similar situations, and it is good in their mind to see it happening to someone else. The laughter might not be malicious. It might be more out of a relief than it is anything else.

More Philosophizing

Alexander Bain

Another philosopher, Alexander Bain, felt that all humor involves degrading something else, similar to what Hobbes thought. However, he tried to expound on that theory a bit and said that the person who is laughing does not even have to be aware of their superiority at the time. He felt that sympathetic laughter was possible, and that it still fit into the basic theory.

In addition, he felt that people were able to laugh at more than just the misfortune of other people. They could laugh at anything they felt superior over, even if it was an idea or ideal rather than a person.

He felt that it was possible for humans to *degrade anything* and to find humor in that degradation. He sounds like a cheery sort of fellow that everyone would want to call a friend.

Henri Bergson

Henri Bergson felt that the ideal for a human would be "elasticity, adaptability, and the thrust of life," and he found things that were the opposite of that funny. Thus, he felt that a person who was rigid and inflexible enough not to change his or her situation was worthy of derision and therefore worthy of laughter, and often contemptuous laughter at that.

He felt superior of people who could not or would not change, and he found those situations humorous.

In essence, he feels that laughter is a way for society to defend against those who refuse to adapt and make changes.

Studies in Recent Times May Contradict the Superiority Theory

Of course, modern research into the Superiority Theory might be throwing a wrench into the philosophy of Plato and the musings of Hobbes and those other philosophers. Instead of people simply laughing when bad things happen to other people, studies today are showing that there might just be a bit more to it than that.

The Boss Says Laugh, You Say How Hard

One of the studies showing that laughter doesn't always have to do with this theory focused on employees and their bosses. In fact, it might be just the opposite. The researchers found that many employees would laugh when their boss was joking and trying to be funny, even if the jokes were less than comedy gold.

Why would they laugh at those jokes? Preservation, more than likely. They wanted to gain the favor of the person in charge, and they would laugh at those jokes in an effort to do just that.

You might be thinking that you would never stoop to such a thing, and that only the desperate would laugh at a boss's joke like that. You might even tell that to your coworkers too. However, look around the room the next time that happens, and you might just be surprised at what you see. Your coworkers are chuckling and, most likely, you are too. Everyone wants to be on good terms with the boss.

Laughing at Everything

As we mentioned earlier in the book, laughter in our daily lives doesn't happen because we are watching comedians and telling one another jokes all the time. Laughter comes from everywhere around us, and even things that many people wouldn't find funny.

Just as comedians see humor in everything, so do regular people. They just do not always know how to express it. Sometimes, it might look like the Superiority Theory at play. Other times, it might be so they can fit in with friends, peers, supervisors, and others in their lives. They even laugh at things that aren't necessarily funny because they want to be accepted and to fit in with the others in the crowd.

Chapter 7

The Incongruity Theory

The basis of the Incongruity Theory is that people will laugh at things that surprise them or whenever something does not adhere to a specific pattern. When you expect something, or have come to believe that you are following an A-A-A pattern, you will feel surprise, and often laugh when you find an A-A-C pattern, or an A-A-C pattern.

It's all about the unexpected when it comes to the Incongruity Theory.

Some who study humor feel that this is the basis of all humor, rather than degradation. As we learn more about the different theories, you will see that many of them contradict one another, naturally. People argue about what is right and what is the real reason we find things funny.

People have been trying to figure this out for thousands of years, and we're not much closer than we were back then. Yet, all of the various theories you will learn about here seem to have valid points and cases. We'll touch more on this later in the book.

Types of Incongruity in Humor

Incongruity can encompass a number of different areas and subjects to find humor, including the following:

Physical Incongruity – You have two or more things that are opposites in some way. For example, Abbott and Costello are certainly an incongruous duo.

Social Incongruity – With this sort of incongruity, you may have a fish out of water, someone who does not "belong" in certain social situations, and humor can ensue from that. A good example might be the movie *Trading Places* with Dan Aykroyd and Eddie Murphy.

Character Incongruity – When a person or character behaves in a manner not consistent with what you know, it can be played for humorous effect. Funnily enough, in a horror film, character incongruity can be played for a rather terrifying effect.

Perspective Incongruity – This relies on misunderstanding and wrong perceptions of the situation, and it is very popular in many different types of comedy. The tense situations in *Three's Company* are a good example – people often had the wrong idea of what was happening based on their perceptions, and that colored how they behaved and what they did.

Solution Incongruity – This relies on someone finding incongruous solutions to their problems. The solutions might not be what the audience expected, but they are in line enough with the reality of the plot that they can work for humor, while keeping the story grounded, if a bit exaggerated.

Philosophies on Incongruity

Immanuel Kant

Immanuel Kant believed that humor stemmed from the "sudden transformation of a strained expectation into nothing." He thought that it was more than mere surprise, as suggested by modern Incongruity theorists. He felt that the change had to be sudden and a large enough change that it caused a shift in emotion. He felt that the change had to be unrealistic in order to elicit laughs.

One of the witticisms of Oscar Wilde fits nicely into this version of the theory. He once said, "Work is the curse of the drinking classes." It subverts the meaning and the expectation in the listener, and that can elicit a laugh.

Herbert Spencer

Herbert Spencer felt that all humor could be "explained as descending incongruity," with descending in this case meaning the descending judgment value. He felt that incongruity needed to have a contract between something dignified and something trivial.

Spencer also felt that incongruity could make humans nervous, and that laughter was the way we got rid of that excess nervousness. It sounds silly, but it might have some basis in truth. Consider the beginning of the book when we talked about a game of hide and seek and how some hiders would start laughing when they saw the person looking for them. Could it be they were laughing because they were nervous? Is laughter nothing more than a relief valve for our tension and nervousness?

What Does the Theory Illustrate?

Some feel that this theory represents finding the appropriate in the inappropriate, or vice versa. Finding those connections between things that might not normally have connections is a part of the humor, a part of the unexpected that so many people seem to enjoy.

At its best, comedy can throw conventions and stereotypes under the bus and make us reexamine our beliefs and the things a group of people, a community, or the world might see as right and wrong. By getting rid of the stereotypes, it might be possible to evolve beyond where we are right now.

This certainly seems like a lofty goal for comedy, and it is. Most comedians don't even feel as though that's something they are aiming for. After all, in this wild and wide world of comedy, anything goes, and sometimes it's not all about changing the world. We have a Gallagher who smashes fruit and gets laughs, so not everything is about huge social changes!

What's Right and Wrong with All of These Comedy Theories?

The theories are malleable, which means people can see and get different things from them. Some might see different reasons to put stock in the Incongruity Theory, while others see another theory as a viable alternative.

Still others may find that there is no single answer, and that humor can be looked at and dissected in many different ways and still be "right" and funny. In fact, there is quite a bit of overlap among all of the theories.

As we go through the rest of the theories, you will see some things that make perfect sense, and you might see some others that don't sit right with you. You aren't alone. Everyone who studies humor has his or her own beliefs, and it can be difficult to get someone to listen to alternate theories. The *best* thing to do is to go through all of these theories with an open mind and see what seems right for you.

A Good Example of the Incongruity Theory

Here's a joke from Groucho Marx that does a good job of illustrating this theory very simply. Watch how it sets up the scene that you picture in your head, and then in the next phrase, it gives you something that you don't expect and that is completely incongruous to what you know can be true. That's where the humor lies.

"One morning I shot an elephant in my pajamas. How he got in my pajamas, I don't know."

Be Careful with Those Jokes

When you see how the jokes work, and you study the Incongruity Theory and try to put it into practice, you may find that it can work out quite well for you. It might not be the only theory out there, and it certainly is not the only one someone interested in humor should study. However, it can give someone a good understanding of how to make some people laugh.

Of course, you have to be very careful with the way that you joke, and you have to be careful with your subject matter. While it is true that this sort of humor has the potential to help "break down those barriers," it is important to think things through.

It is possible to go too far and to stray so far over the line of blue comedy that the comedian, the joke, or the story actually becomes offensive and repulsive to an audience.

There needs to be enough time and distance in order for the joke to be funny. For example, joking about race and sexual stereotypes can be fine unless they cross that line into actual racism or sexism. For the sake of good taste, and to keep the peace between the comedian and his or her audience, it is important not to cross that line.

Chapter 8

The Mechanical Theory

Do you remember Henri Bergson from a couple of chapters back? He's in Chapter 7, if you want to refresh your memory, or you can keep reading and we'll refresh it right here. Bergson was a proponent of the Superiority Theory, but he went a step further and said that humor could come from the rigidity and inflexibility of certain people, or even certain social conventions.

Bergson's Theory

In his work *Laughter*, Bergson wondered just what laughter meant, and he tried to analyze it as best he could, even though most feel his theory and most theories aren't entirely correct. One of the issues with what Bergson was doing, and the others who came up with their own theories for that matter, was the limits they placed on themselves.

They seemed to have come into the research with minds already made up of what they thought was funny and why they thought it was funny without ever looking at the big picture and all of the variables.

For example, Bergson said that:

Laughter is Human

He meant that we laughed only at people and the things that they did or created. This seems to be a rather narrow approach, but perhaps what he really meant was that we laugh at what is human, as well as those things in the natural world that may reflect part of our own human nature. Even then, he may not have been entirely correct in his thinking.

Laughter is Cerebral and Distant

Bergson also felt that laughter was something that needed distance. He felt that people needed to have a detached attitude in order to laugh at something and to find it funny. Again, this seems to be very limiting and actually wrong.

Consider sarcasm. Most people who laugh at sarcastic humor in real life are actually quite close to the subjects of the ridicule – it could be their friends and their family they are making fun of, albeit in a loving and caring way most of the time.

Many people can laugh at themselves and the foolish things they've done, and they can see that they've done something silly. This seems to fly in the face of his theory.

Laughter Has a Social Function

Bergson is right about this. Laughter can make groups of people feel more at ease and it can make them feel happier. However, he feels that laughter is simply a social gesture rather than having any psychological or physiological connection. He felt that laughter would serve societal needs.

He also felt that society would naturally organize people into different categories or groups, and that the people who were in those groups would adopt or develop the characteristics of said group.

Those people who can't adopt or who choose not to change are the elements of humor – they are *mechanical* in the way they approach each day, so they just can't make the changes necessary to fit into the societal machine.

I Like Me the Way I Am

People who did not change and who were steadfast in their ways, despite the need for change that everyone else around them could see, could be funny. They could also be quite tragic and damaged characters if the circumstances surrounding them weren't played for laughs.

Those who study humor call this the Mechanical Theory, and it is indeed an offshoot of the Superiority Theory. After all, when you see a character that you know should make changes in order to be successful at something or simply to make their lives easier, most people do feel a bit superior.

It's All the Same

Let's look at some of the characters from television shows that will fit into this theory of comedy.

Homer Simpson and Others Who D'oh Not Want to Change

The Simpsons has been on the air for decades now, and everyone's favorite lovable oaf is still pretty much the same guy he was when the show started. In fact, quite a few of the characters on this show, as well as many animated shows and sitcoms, follow this path. According to Bergson's Mechanical Theory, since Homer doesn't change and still gets into trouble and predicaments due to the same behaviors, humor will ensue.

It does, but it might not always be due to Homer's rigidity and resistance to changing and being a better person. Other elements certainly go into the writing of the show to help provide humor.

Once again, it seems as though this theory of comedy might be partially right, but it doesn't have *all* of the answers.

One of the reasons that characters on television shows don't change is because people come to expect certain things from them.

Other Television Shows with Characters Who Don't Change

- South Park
- Family Guy
- American Dad
- Malcolm in the Middle
- Three's Company
- The Dick Van Dyke Show

This list can go on and on, too. You could probably rattle off some of your favorite comedies and see just how rigid those characters are from one episode to the next and from one season to the next. This is true with many of the older shows. They adhered to formula very strictly.

Mechanical Theory in Other Media

Consider some characters in film that just don't change, too. While it can be more difficult, since most movies are only a couple of hours long, you can see this when a movie is a series. While *James Bond* films might not be comedy, the titular character certainly doesn't change much from one movie to the next.

It happens in series of books, not to mention comic books, as well. Characters can go for several books without making all of the changes they should make in their lives based on the experiences and circumstances they've been through in the previous books. It is not limited to comedy, and it is certainly not limited to television.

However, and this is a big however, things are not always that way. Times they are a-changing, and that can be a very good thing.

Times Are Changing and the Theory May Be Losing More Steam

The world's attitude toward media is changing, and the things that people consumed and loved during the '60s through the millennium, with characters that don't grow and change, are slowly going away.

Of course, this isn't happening with all shows, but you *can* see character growth – however slow it might be – in shows such as *The Big Bang Theory* and *How I Met Your Mother*. The changes do not happen quickly, and they are taking place over many seasons, but there is change and growth. The humor is still there though, which may well contradict Bergson's rigid theory.

Peoples' tastes change, and they want to see more growth in the characters they come to know and love. There will always be a place for those characters whom are so mechanical they can't change, but they do not seem to be the staple they once were.

Chapter 9

The Benign Violation Theory

The Benign Violation Theory is a relative newcomer when it comes to the theory of humor. Developed by Dr. Peter McGraw and Caleb Warren, the theory is still undergoing testing in Boulder, Colorado, at the Humor Research Lab. Yes, there is such a place, and they use the acronym HuRL.

The Basis of the Benign Violation Theory

According to the developers of the theory, humor will only occur when a situation meets three specific requirements:

First, there must be a threat of some sort. It needs to threaten the way one sees the world or one's morals, or it could even be a physical threat.

Second, the threatening situation must actually be benign, so there is no real danger of actual harm.

Third, the person has to see both the first and the second requirement at the same time.

The researchers feel that something is funny when it seems harmful or threatening in some manner, but it turns out to be harmless.

How Does the Theory Work with Different Types of Humor?

Let's look at a few of the different types of humor out there and see if the Benign Violation Theory fits.

I've Fallen and I Can't Get Up

If someone trips and falls or receives some type of injury, it doesn't seem as though it's a laughing matter at all, but we've already discussed how we often laugh at these things. However, it's only when we know that the other person is okay that we start to laugh. If the person received an actual injury, it goes quickly from comedy into the realm of tragedy.

Most likely, the first type of "comedy" was from accidental slapstick, along with humorous violations that could have the initial perception of a threat. This might include tickling and even the sort of play fighting the children often do.

Did You Hear the One About the...

As humans slowly started to become more sophisticated and wear things other than loincloths, the type of humor changed. The theory proposes that other violations, such as violations to societal norms, linguistic norms, moral norms, and even personal dignity would become humorous to those who perceived a threat to those things and then realize that the threats are actually benign.

This theory can also fit in with other types of humor, including blue humor. The joke starts out appearing as though it is trading on social or moral violations, or even violations against someone's dignity, and then the punch line or resolution turns out to be benign.

This is why many different types of jokes can be funny. A bit later in the chapter, we'll also look at how this theory can help to explain why some things might not be funny in some situations.

Now That's What I Call Punny

Puns, whether you love them or hate them, are a part of the world's humor collective today. They are a violation of linguistics, and they are certainly harmless, so they can fit nicely into this theory. Many people enjoy puns, but you have to admit that they are often worthy of a few groans.

So, naturally, we'll include ten of the most groan-worthy right here for your pleasure or disdain.

10 Puns for Work, School, and Other Places Where You Want People to Shake Their Heads at You

A chicken crossing the road is poultry in motion

Time flies like an arrow. Fruit flies like a banana

Corduroy pillows are making headlines

A horse is a very stable animal

A dog that gave birth to puppies near the road was ticketed for littering

A bicycle can't stand alone because it is two-tired

Show me a piano falling down a mineshaft and I'll show you A-flat minor

Without geometry, life is pointless

The shoe said to the hat, "You go on ahead, I'll follow on foot"

If you don't pay your exorcist, you get repossessed

Now, take these "gems," go out, and entertain the masses!

Other Methods of Benign Violation

According to McGraw and Warren, violations can occur in other ways as well. They feel that humor can come when the violation seems "benign if one norm suggests something is wrong but another salient norm suggests it is acceptable."

They go on to state that "a violation can also seem benign when one is psychologically distant from the violation or is only weakly committed to the violated norm."

What these two statements are saying is that something can be funny with enough distance and with the right point of view.

Psychological distance can actually be one of the most important elements of what people find funny and what they think is a tragedy. A quote from Mel Brooks sums it up nicely. He said, "Tragedy is when I cut my finger. Comedy is when you walk into an open sewer and die."

When Things Aren't Funny

So, the theory proposes that it can see why things are funny, and that following those rules will generally result in something being funny. Of course, by now we know there are quite a few different elements that can go into humor, and one theory doesn't necessarily fit everything.

However, the Benign Violation Theory actually does a rather good job of explaining why quite a few things aren't funny.

The humor can fail when it is trying to illustrate a situation that does not have a simultaneous feeling of being a violation while also being benign. For example, a physical violation might actually turn violent if it becomes too aggressive.

Another reason that comedy might not work is that the jokes don't strike the right balance. They are either too tame or too risqué. Going too far in either direction can mean failure. Thus, the violation implied is no longer a benign violation.

These seem to be accurate, and they do apply well to the Benign Violation Theory. That might not mean that the theory is perfect, though. After all, the researchers who propose this theory are still experimenting and observing.

How Does Benign Violation Compare to Veatch's Theory of Humor?

In 1998, years before the Benign Violation Theory came into the world, a man named Thomas C. Veatch presented his theory on humor in the International Journal of Humor Research. He felt that his was a complete theory of humor. It also has three conditions that one must meet.

We'll look at his three conditions, and if you've been paying attention to this chapter, you will notice something very similar. Here are Veatch's requirements from his own website:

"Something is wrong. The perceiver thinks that things in a situation ought to be a certain way – and cares about that – and is violated."

"The situation is actually okay. That is, the perceiver has in mind a predominating view of the situation as being normal."

"Both occur at the same time. That is, the normal and the violation understandings are present in the mind of the perceiver at the same instant."

Didn't We Just Cover That?

Did you catch that? His requirements are the *same exact requirements* as Benign Violation Theory. Keep in mind that Veatch's theory was around years before the BV Theory. It makes one wonder why people suddenly think that it is "new" now that it has a different label on it from different researchers.

Veatch's Favorite Example of the Theory in Action

He feels that one of the best ways to see this in action is with a simple game of peek-a-boo with a child. Children are open to the world and do not have preconceived notions of comedy and what is funny, and the game is actually something practiced all around the world, so there are no real cultural barriers with it. The laughter elicited during the game is therefore pure and not forced.

Let's look at how the little ones perceive this game.

First, they see their mom or dad's smiling face right in front of them. This is the normal for the baby.

Second, the tricky parent moves out of the field of view or covers his or her face, thus vanishing right before the child's eyes as if by sorcery. The baby has no idea what happened – it's a baby, they aren't that smart yet so give the poor thing a break.

Then, third, mom or dad suddenly returns and… the baby laughs and giggles. All is right with the world again, and it happens so fast that the baby is happy again before the violation – the disappearance of a parent – can make a negative impact.

Slow parents who take their sweet time with the game might actually find that the children cry. If they take too long "returning," the child will worry. The "violation" takes hold. On the other hand, if the parent doesn't take enough time with peek-a-boo, the game loses the fun for the child. This is just like going too far or not far enough with a joke.

This is a simple game, but it always brings about the laughter and the smiles. It also conforms very nicely to Veatch's theory and the Benign Violation Theory, which, come on, seems to be a repackaged version of Veatch's theory.

Chapter 10

The Relief, or Release, Theory

It is really not much of a surprise that the proponent of the Release Theory, or Relief Theory, of humor would be Sigmund Freud. He was a man bent on the idea of "release," and yes, that's a double-entendre. While he did not develop this basic theory, he did quite a bit to reinforce it. He wrote about this in his work "Jokes and Their Relation to the Unconscious."

He believed that laughter and humor could act as a form of release from societal repressions, sexual repressions, pent-up emotions, and more. You will remember that Herbert Spencer, from earlier in the book, thought the same thing and felt that laughter was a way to release tension, frustration, and even anger.

So *That's* Why We Have World Peace!
Sure, there is some validity that laughing can make you feel happy and that it can help you to reduce your tension. However, if laughter could take away everyone's anger and frustrations, the world would be a much kinder and happier place. We wouldn't fight, shoot one another, or go to war. Comedy and humor are great, but they can't

fix everything and the world doesn't suddenly get better just because you can find a "release."

Build the Tension and Then Release It

The theory tries to describe humor as needing a tension-and-release model. There must first be a buildup of tension and then the relief comes along with the punch line. This was something Spencer adamantly believed, but he was not able to explain why other things – puns, witticisms, and actual jokes – were funny. They did not last long enough to build up any actual tension.

Freud went on to expound on the theory and on humor. He did not believe that humor came from a feeling of superiority. He did not feel that it could come from awareness of incongruity, either. He believed it was all about the removal of tension, and that was where the laughter came from.

He felt there were three sources of laughter:

Joking

The Comic

Humorous

Freud believed that when "joking," the saved energy would help to repress sexual feelings or anger, and it would release with laughter.

He felt that the "comic" (cartoons in this case, not stand-ups) required cognitive energy to solve the intellectual challenge of the joke, and the release of that energy was laughter.

Finally, the "humorous" was a way of saving emotional energy. He said that the emotional energy we might have been building for some crisis could turn into laughter when that crisis turned out to be a non-threat.

Does This Sound Confusing?

Freud's theory, while believed wholeheartedly by many, has some flaws in it. In fact, it has quite a few. He talks about saving energy for different things, but how this happens is not clear. He does not explore it in his writing, either. It seems as though it would make more sense to say that the person did not use any energy rather than they saved energy.

He also never went into detail about just how one would differentiate between their "saved energy" and their "free energy."

Would you be getting ready to laugh and then realize you were low on comic energy so you'd better not finish that comic?

Would using your energy correctly be inherent, an evolved trait you would not even have to think about when using it? The latter seems the most likely, but the semantics used in the discussion of the theory make it shaky at best.

What Else Did Freud Think About Humor?

Freud thought of humor as trying to "outwit the censor." He thought it was a way to relieve oneself of all the restraints they felt and that it allowed them to be closer to the natural impulses of humans – good and bad.

Some feel that his theory can explain why some ostensibly bad characters in comedy could be loved, as well as why so many men and women have a penchant for off-color jokes.

Freud believed that the internal censor we all have would not normally allow us to laugh at such things. The only way to do that was to trick the censor and to use various elements of humor to do that. According to him, puns were a way to do this, and so was misrepresentation.

Humor and Dreams

We all know that Freud was into dream interpretation as much as he was into believing most things were about sexual repression. He felt that there were actually quite a few similarities between how our dream thoughts become distorted and how techniques of humor work to trick the internal censor. He found that dreams were another way to take down the FCC of the mind.

How Wrong Is the Relief Theory?

The Relief Theory doesn't have to be entirely wrong. In fact, there is relief from tension when we laugh at jokes. We find relief as the tension of the joke itself diminishes with the punch line, and we find it happens to be a good way to relieve the actual physical tension that we have. In that sense, it is true.

However, to say that all humor has to derive from the tension and then release formula is not correct in all cases. As mentioned, there is no tension buildup when reading a simple comic strip, and many jokes are quick enough that they don't require the buildup of actual tension. Freud himself was a fan of puns, and they are certainly tension-free… unless someone keeps telling you puns constantly.

By the way, when the investor came home from work, he was spent.

Chapter 11:

Freud, Aristotle, and Archie Bunker: Or What's Up with Those Theories Over There?

O ver the past several chapters, we've gone over a variety of different theories of comedy:

Superiority

Incongruity

Mechanical

Benign Violation

Relief

Each of the theories purports to be the one true theory on humor. They claim to tell you precisely how to discover what is funny. However, you've probably noticed the deficiencies in all of these different theories. They all have their good points and they can actually explain some types of humor quite well.

When you look at them, you can't actually see any of them explaining *all* of the different kinds of humor. The Superiority Theory touted by Aristotle and Plato works well when we are laughing at some of the mishaps and misfortunes of people around us and at comedians telling stories of their own failings. However, that theory doesn't really explain why people find puns funny.

On the other hand, Incongruity Theory does explain those things. It comes in to help deal with many of the elements and types of humor that don't fit with Superiority Theory. Then you have Mechanical, Benign Violation, and the Relief Theory that Freud loved so very much.

While there might be some overlap, you need to realize that all of these theories have something to offer and that none of them is entirely correct.

Missing the Punch Line

The best humor is simple and doesn't need explanation. That doesn't mean that it is simple, though. In fact, when you get down to it, humor is actually quite complex, especially considering that it is universal among humans.

The current theories that we have to explain humor just don't do a thorough enough job of explaining humor and none of them (apologies to Freud and his nervous excessive psychic energy) can truly explain why you can go from understanding a joke to laughing and cackling like a mad person.

Look at one of the most popular and successful comedies of all time, *All in the Family*. The show incorporates many different sorts of humor successfully, including puns, misunderstandings, blue humor, and so much more. It is a veritable stew of comedy and it defies classification into any single category or humor theory.

Will There Ever Be a Unifying Theory of Comedy?

One of the big questions is whether you will ever hear about a unifying theory, something that can explain all different sorts of humor and explain just why we laugh at things. Chances are slim that this will ever happen, no matter how hard people try.

Free for All

So, no one really knows anything about comedy.

Well, that's not true at all. There are actually quite a few experts out there on comedy. They don't need to have a degree, and they don't need to study all of the works of the ancient Greek philosophers to try to enlighten themselves on the fine art of funny. You are an expert. If you like to laugh, and you know what makes *you* laugh, then you are your very own expert.

If you don't like puns, avoid them like the plague. If blue humor makes you nervous and you don't like it, avoid it. Everyone should find the types of humor that they like and embrace them. Humor makes you feel good, and whatever it is that makes you laugh can be a great thing for your psyche and your health.

When it comes to humor, Archie Bunker from *All in the Family* has an apt quote. "One man's goose is another man's dander." Just like what you like, and don't always try too hard to define it.

Chapter 12

Humor as a Defense Mechanism

Humor can do quite a few things for you, just as we mentioned all the way back in the first chapter. However, quite a few people actually utilize humor as a defense mechanism, and this is common enough that it actually warrants a few pages of its own. Using humor as defense can be good and bad.

The Truth Behind the Defense

Why do people use humor as a defense mechanism? People that do this, according to psychologists, often have low self-esteem, or they are trying to deal with some very real and very tragic issues. Many times, they will use humor in an effort to deflect the feelings they may have against themselves, or the way they perceive themselves (and therefore feel that others perceive them).

They can do this in a number of different ways.

The Self-Deprecating Humorist

This is one of the top ways that people use humor as a defense. They figure that they will beat the others to the punch with the jokes about themselves. If they feel that they are overweight, then they will talk about their weight and make fun of themselves. By making fun before others can do it, they take away the power from others who might say something about their weight.

This works for many different areas of life, from weight to relationship status, family status, and more. Most of the time, using humor as a defense like this is a way the people can deal with what they feel is a tragedy of some sort.

By using humor, they feel as though they can protect themselves from whatever it is in the world that is hurting them.

How Do They Do It?

How do people get into the practice of using this type of humor as a defense? They should not take things seriously, and they always look for the humorous things in what they do and they will be the first ones to mention it, just so they can beat everyone to making fun of them.

Sometimes, they could be considered the class clown, or to have the class-clown personality if they are an adult. Sometimes this can go too far. Having a good sense of humor and learning to laugh at things you do can be a good thing.

Learning to brush off the things that other people might say is a good thing too. Ignoring those who don't have anything constructive to offer you is a good defense mechanism, and it can be a healthy one to pair with humor.

Falling Back on Sarcasm

Just as popular as self-deprecating humor is sarcasm. However, it takes a very different approach. Instead of the person making fun of themselves, they look for the flaws and problems in others around them and use those things as barbs and bullets against people.

In the beginning, they might only use sarcasm to defend when someone else says something about them or to them. This can change quickly, though. As someone becomes more adept at sarcasm and feels more comfortable using it, it can become a part of their personality. That is not usually a good thing.

Many people don't like being around someone who is constantly caustically sarcastic. It grates on the nerves and people don't like to be on the receiving end of it. This can mean the person who falls back to sarcasm all the time might actually lose family and friends.

Good or Bad?

When you examine these different types of mechanisms for defense, you can see that they are actually quite dark. No matter how funny they might be on the outside, there is definitely a darkness roiling just beneath the surface, and that's sad.

Having a good and healthy sense of humor is a good thing. When you use humor as defense, and make fun of the silly things you do, it's okay. In fact, it's natural. Quite a few people do this.

However, when someone is harboring deep sadness, self-esteem issues, or even self-loathing, humor is just a mask and all of the problems still exist underneath. When someone uses humor as their sole method of dealing with a reality they do not like, it is unhealthy.

Of course, it's not always that simple. Sometimes there is quite a bit more going on, as you will see. Sometimes there is no other way. Humor is a tool one can use for good or for bad.

When It's the Only Choice

Sometimes, humor as a defense can be the only way to make it through a difficult situation. In those instances, humor as defense can be very good for people.

Look at some of the following examples.

Humor in the Holocaust

During the Holocaust, many of the Jews in Europe had to develop a sense of humor in the face of death just to make it through each day with their sanity. Much of the humor developed during that time was gallows humor because of the situation. Many who made it out of the concentration camps said that if it weren't for using humor as their defense, they might well have committed suicide.

Laughter in the Face of Darkness

People who are in highly stressful professions, such as frontline military and law enforcement, as well as people in the medical field, develop similar senses of humor. They are looking for ways to deal with the things they see and struggle with every day.

Most people who see and hear this type of humor will not get it. It's often morbid and dark, and it only is funny to those who are in those positions. However, it provides the necessary release and catharsis that those individuals need.

Professions that Use Humor for Defense

Police officer

Detective

Mortician

Medical examiner

Military member

EMT

Fireman

Psychologist

Prison guard

These are only a few of the various professions that have to see and deal with the darker side of human nature on a regular basis. It is no wonder they fall back on humor to make it from one day to the next.

When you consider the rate of mental health issues, family problems, alcoholism, and more that people in those professions face, you can see why it is important to find a way to laugh at everything that's happening.

Use Humor the Right Way

Humor is a powerful tool, and you need to use it wisely. This simply means that people shouldn't use humor as the sole means of dealing with the other issues that might be plaguing them. There is no shame in finding professional help to deal with mental health issues that people might be using humor to mask.

Chapter 13

The Evolution of Comedy

In this chapter, we'll go through a brief – very brief – history of comedy. To start, we'll go back in time a bit. Actually, we'll go just about *all the way back*.

In the Beginning

Comedy has very likely been around since the very first people, right when we were coming down out of the trees. The first laugh, one that wasn't based in tickling or play, was probably at the expense of some poor caveman sporting a unibrow who fell off a rock or was scared of his loud and unexpected expulsion of gas. That's right, the first comedy was probably all about slapstick and fart jokes.

Of course, there's a chance that this is off-base and that the reality is that one of Jerry Seinfeld's ancient relatives stood in front of his fellow cave dwellers and asked, "What's up with these wooly mammoths?"

As the social skills of these early humans started to grow, change, and mature, it is likely that the humor in those early tribes started to mature as well. This didn't happen overnight, though.

It's Greek to Me

Time passes, comedy starts to change, and along come the Greeks to give it a real kick in the pants. However, the comedy of the Greeks is not the same modern comedy we have today.

Comedy was one of the three forms of drama, along with tragedy and the satyr play. Strange as it sounds, the satyr play, which features a burlesque chorus of satyrs, was not pure comedy. The Greeks considered it a tragicomedy instead.

The Greeks divide their comedy, Athenian comedy, into three periods:

Old Comedy

Middle Comedy

New Comedy

Old Comedy

Perhaps the best known from this type of comedy is Aristophanes. He created some biting political satire, along with innuendo. He

would make fun of many of the most famous personalities in his day, including Socrates. It is possible to see how this type of comedy influenced others down through history, including the writings of Voltaire and Swift. A bit farther along the historical line, you can see the influence of this type of comedy in satires such as *Dr. Strangelove* and even *Saturday Night Live.*

Middle Comedy

Middle Comedy, generally referred to as coming after Aristophanes and his contemporaries, is quite a bit different from Old Comedy, where the chorus played a role in the plot. They no longer impersonated public characters on the stage, and instead they ridiculed and made fun of other, general things rather than personal things. They focused on ridiculing the literary rather than political.

Unfortunately, there are no complete Middle Comedies available, so it is difficult for scholars to tell just how good or impressive the plays might have been.

New Comedy

New Comedy really started after the death of Alexander the Great and lasted all the way through the reign of the Macedonians. The three most famous playwrights of the day were Menander, Philemon, and Diphilus. The plays created by these three, while vastly different, are similar to what we might call sitcoms today. They were very popular in their day.

Shakespearean and Elizabethan Comedy

You probably wouldn't recognize this as comedy, at least not by the standards we have today. They have a different tone and a different feel, and the elements of humor might be very light in these plays. With Shakespeare in particular, a comedy was something that had a happy ending, a much lighter tone, and would usually have a marriage.

Vaudeville

From about the 1880s all the way through the 1930s, vaudeville was a popular type of entertainment that included a number of different acts on the same bill. There were many different sorts of acts in a vaudeville production, including musicians, magicians, jugglers, one-act plays, celebrities, dancers, and yes, comedians.

It might surprise you to learn that a number of comedians that you know and love from television actually had their start in vaudeville. Some of the names you will probably recognize include:

- Jack Benny

- Buster Keaton

- The Marx Brothers

- Jimmy Durante

- Abbot and Costello

- Bob Hope

- Red Skelton

Many of these performers came in at the end of the vaudeville area and transitioned to television and to film. Others started in the earlier days of vaudeville and saw that it was a bit easier to make a living on screen than it was on the stage.

The Silent Film and Beyond

Film changed everything for comedy. From the silent film artists such as Charlie Chaplin all the way to Dean Martin and Jerry Lewis, The Three Stooges, and modern comedians such as George Carlin, Eddie Murphy, and Robin Williams, film and television brought comedy to anyone who wanted it – and that was just about everyone.

Today, from stage to screen to page, there is a near-endless supply of comedy for you to enjoy.

Chapter 14

Comedy on Stage, Television, and Film: Things to Learn From, or: the Chapter of Awesome Lists

In this chapter, we're going to cover some of the (subjectively) best comedy of all time. We'll look a variety of different mediums and provide the reader, that's you, with suggestions on things to watch, listen to, or read.

Are you going to like all of these comedians? Will you love all of the movies and television shows suggested? No, you probably won't, and *that's actually the point.*

You can consider the suggestions in this chapter to be your homework. You are exposing yourself to types of comedy that you might not have seen or known before, and some you might not necessarily like. However, this will broaden your horizons, and you may find some great new shows, films, or comedians that you love.

Comedy on Television: Yesterday and Today

The following are some of the best and most beloved comedies on television, and they are well worth watching just to see what you do and don't find funny. Make sure you give each of the series a chance and watch several episodes to get into the swing of their individual rhythms before giving up on them.

Some you will like, and some you won't. Some, you will actually detest with a passion generally reserved for stubbing your toe. One of the things you *will* find, though, is that you have a better understanding of the different types of humor used in each of these shows, and you can now actually see the blend of different comedic elements.

30 Rock

The Andy Griffith Show

Arrested Development

The Big Bang Theory

The Brady Bunch

The Bugs Bunny Looney Tunes Comedy Hour

The Daily Show with John Stewart

The Dick Van Dyke Show

Family Guy

Fawlty Towers

Friends

Gilligan's Island

The Honeymooners

How I Met Your Mother

It's Always Sunny in Philadelphia

Louie

M*A*S*H

Modern Family

Monty Python's Flying Circus

Parks and Recreation

Scrubs

Seinfeld

The Simpsons

South Park

Three's Company

Comedy in the Cinema

Just as with the television shows, you will find some movies here you have probably already seen and love. You will find some that you've never seen and now love. You will also find some that will make you shake your head and wonder why you just wasted two hours of your life.

Still, it's worth it to give all of the movies a chance. Everything you consume informs you of what you find funny and what you don't, and this enables you to learn more about humor and why some people find even the most repugnant and silly movies on the list funny.

Abbot & Costello Meet Frankenstein

Airplane

Anchorman: The Legend of Ron Burgundy

Arthur

The Big Lebowski

Blazing Saddles

Bridesmaids

Caddyshack

Coming to America

Dr. Strangelove or: How I Learned to Stop Worrying and Love the Bomb

Ghostbusters

The Hangover

The Jerk

M*A*S*H

Monty Python and the Holy Grail

National Lampoon's Animal House

Office Space

Raising Arizona

Stripes

There's Something About Mary

This Is Spinal Tap

Tootsie

Trading Places

Waiting for Guffman

Wet Hot American Summer

Comedy on the Page

Who says you have to see and hear something for it to be funny? You can read humor just as easily, and you let your mind and your imagination, along with your incredible comprehension skills, do all of the work for you. The books in this section cover the gamut, from memoirs to novels.

Born Standing Up by Steve Martin

Bossypants by Tina Fey

Comedy at the Edge: How Stand-up in the 1970s Changed America by Richard Zoglin

The Comedy Writer by Peter Farrelly

Gasping for Airtime: Two Years in the Trenches of Saturday Night Live by Jay Mohr

Good Omens by Terry Pratchett and Neil Gaiman

Great Comedians Talk about Comedy by Larry Wilde

How to Sharpen Pencils by David Rees

I Am America (And So Can You!) by Stephen Colbert

I Like You: Hospitality Under the Influence by Amy Sedaris

Is Everyone Hanging Out Without Me? And Other Concerns by Mindy Kaling

John Dies at the End by David Wong

Live from New York: An Uncensored History of Saturday Night Live, as Told by Its Stars, Writers, and Guests by Tom Shales and James Andrew Miller

Lost in the Funhouse: The Life and Mind of Andy Kaufman by Bill Zehme

M*A*S*H by Richard Hooker

Me Talk Pretty One Day by David Sedaris

On the Real Side: A History of African American Comedy by Mel Watkin

The Onion Book of Known Knowledge: A Definitive Encyclopedia of Existing Information by The Onion

The Pro by Garth Ennis

SCTV: Behind the Scenes by Dave Thomas

The Second City Almanac of Improvisation by Anne Libera and Second City Inc.

Show Me the Funny!: At the Writers' Table with Hollywood's Top Comedy Writers by Peter Desberg and Jeffrey Davis

The Will to Whatevs: A Guide to Modern Life by Eugene Mirman

Without Feathers by Woody Allen

Zombie Spaceship Wasteland by Patton Oswalt

You may have noticed by now that *M*A*S*H* is in three different categories here – television, movies, and books. That's because it really is that good and it appeals to many people. Try it in each of its different forms so you can get a better idea of how the style and tone of the comedy changes from one to the other.

Don't limit the types of things you read, either. You can find great humor in many different areas that use the written word including the comics in the newspaper, comic books, bathroom stalls, and much more.

In addition to the books listed above, you might want to consider some books on the craft of creating comedy.

The following are five great choices you will want to consider if you want to know more about creating and writing comedy:

Comedy Writing Secrets by Mel Helitzer and Mark Shatz

The Complete Idiot's Guide to Writing Comedy by James Mendrinos

The Joke's On You: How to Write Comedy by Stephen Hoover

The New Comedy Writing Step by Step by Gene Perret

Writing the Comedy Blockbuster: The Inappropriate Goal by Keith Giglio

In the next chapter, we will go into the basics of comedy writing as well as what it takes to get started.

Comedy on the Stage

One of the earliest forms of comedy was to have one person tell jokes to or amuse another person or a group of people. That formula was so popular we've even built entire buildings, clubs if you will, to enjoy this.

Here are twenty-five excellent stand-up comedians. Some are still with us and working today and you might even get to see them live. Others are performing at the big Comedy Club in the Sky, but you can find their performances on DVD, YouTube, and elsewhere.

Andy Kaufman

Aziz Ansari

Bob Newhart

Bobcat Goldthwait

Chris Rock

Dave Attell

Dave Chappelle

Don Rickles

Eddie Murphy

George Carlin

Jackie Mason

Jerry Seinfeld

Joe Rogan

Johnny Carson

Lenny Bruce

Louis C.K.

Milton Berle

Redd Foxx

Richard Pryor

Roseanne Barr

Sarah Silverman

Stephen Wright

Steve Martin

Tracy Morgan

Zach Galifianakis

This is merely a handful of the comedians you can explore, and this list is sure to cause some arguments. You might be wondering where some of your favorites are. The comedians included on the list to cover a wide range of different styles, and that's why you might not see some of your favorites. This list is not a "best of" or a complete list by any means, so take a deep breath and relax.

What this list does do though is provide you with some solid comedy.

Is That It?

Are these the only shows you need to watch and the only books you should read if you want to learn more about comedy and the theories of what make people laugh? No, not by a long shot.

This is just the beginning.

This chapter is a nice primer of one hundred different things (plus the five bonus books) you can try so you can get a rounded self-education in comedy. It's not even scratching the surface, though. People have been being funny for thousands of years. Tons of other great media and comedians are out there just waiting for you to discover them.

Chapter 15

The Basics of Comedy Writing

In this chapter, we will look at some of the rules of comedy writing that stand-up comedians, as well as sitcom, sketch, movie, book, and other types of writers. Each of these techniques is tried and true, and each is something you can employ when you are writing comedy, and when you are trying to learn more about the form.

Play on Words

Language, and the audience's ability to understand the language, is vital in much of comedy. Creating a scene that uses pratfalls and slapstick only can be funny at first, but it can grow tired rather quickly. That's why jokes that utilize plays on words are very popular and account for quite a bit of the comedy we know and enjoy.

People like plays on words because they are relatively simply to understand. They utilize some of the famous phrases and clichés that we heard as we were growing up, and they twist those clichés into something new, fresh, and funny.

One of the most often-cited examples of this is the phrase "The way to a man's heart is through his stomach." However, Roseanne Barr gave it her iconic twist when she said, "The quickest way to a man's heart is through his chest."

This technique and type of humor has been around a long time, and some might say that it can get a bit stale. People love it though, and when you can create new plays on words and phrases, it is possible to keep this type of comedy fresh and fun.

Specificity

The joke or story that the writer is creating needs to be specific instead of being general. It is able to draw people into the story far more easily, and they can picture it in their minds. Instead of telling someone you were in a car, you can let the audience know the model. Instead of saying the word "dog," you could use a specific breed.

Always be as specific as possible. It clarifies the story, and it helps to make things quite a bit funnier in most cases.

Think about some of your favorite comedies and you will see this is true.

Always Put the Funny at the End

The punch line comes at the end for a reason, and you should make sure you always put the funny words at the end when you can. Rearranging the sentence, whether for written comedy or for stand-up, often works best when you have the funniest words or phrases at the end. The comedian leads the people along through the joke or the story and then lands it at the last second.

What Words Are Funny?

You've probably heard people say that some words sound funnier than others do. This is actually very true, as strange as it might seem. Words that have a hard "C" or a hard "K" are generally thought of as being quite potent, funny words when used in a comedic context. Of course, words with those sounds aren't the only funny words in the English language, but they are quite good.

Here's a list of great words that sound funny, and that really can work quite well when utilized properly in comedy:

Canoodle

Cantankerous

Cockamamie

Collywobbles

Comeuppance

Fuddy-duddy

Gobbledygook

Hoosegow

Jackanapes

Kerfuffle

Klutz

Malarkey

Mugwump

Ornery

Rambunctious

Shenanigan

Skedaddle

Troglodyte

Vomitory

Yahoo

There you have a list of twenty words considered by Dr. Robert Beard to be among the funniest in the world. Notice just how many of them have hard "C" and "K" sounds in them.

Let it Come Naturally

One of the issues that some new to writing comedy have is that they are writing toward their joke or their punch line. They just want to get to that point, and that often means the setup will fail and the overall joke will fall flat.

Instead of creating a joke or a scene to lead toward the gag or punch line, the best comedy writers take situations, characters, and the like and then see what happens naturally, and write the jokes from those situations. They look for the conflict in the scene or with the situation, and *that* is where they find the comedy.

They seem to find that it is much easier to do this way rather than trying to shoehorn in a joke. Everything comes off sounding natural rather than sounding forced – and that's always a good thing.

Don't Overwrite

A tendency of some writers who are new to writing – whether it is comedy or something else entirely – is to overwrite. They think that more is better, and this rarely is the case. The writing should only be as long as it needs to be and not a word longer. If you can get the joke across in ten words rather than a hundred words, it might be better that way.

Of course, there are some exceptions to this rule. Those who tell longer stories for their comedy may need to write more. Still, all of the words *need to be necessary* for that particular comic style. Writing briefly is a skill that it takes many people quite a long time to develop.

Repetition and Callbacks

Repetition is very important in most forms of comedy today. When you watch a movie, or a sitcom, you can easily see when things are repeat, or have a callback from earlier in the narrative and each time

– as long as the writer doesn't go overboard – the laughs are bigger. Generally, the writers will use the Rule of Three. The same action or setup might be repeated two times, and the big joke will come on the third time.

Repetition does a few things for the writer. It serves to build the final joke over a longer period. It also helps to get the audience to see what is happening, to build their tension, and to give them the relief they need at the end of the joke. It also helps to make them feel a bit like an insider. They know what's happening.

Callbacks themselves don't even have to be particularly funny to work. Since the writer set up the callback at the end, thanks to the jokes and stories from earlier, the audience accepts it and it will generally get a laugh because people *get* it.

Interestingly, if someone comes in during the latter portion of a show and sees *only* the callback, he or she will not generally laugh – unless they feel coerced by the rest of the crowd. The reason for this is simple. They have no idea what's happening; they are not insiders like the rest of the audience.

It's All Good

Comedy covers many different areas, as we've seen through the course of this book. That means that nothing should be "off-limits" as long as the writer knows his or her audience or intended audience.

Pushing the boundaries is a tried and true tradition in comedy, and that is just how it should be. Consider the things comedians such as Sarah Silverman, George Carlin, and Richard Pryor said and did. Consider some of the best skits on *Saturday Night Live* that push the envelope.

Comedians need to be as fearless and bold as anyone who writes. They need to test the boundaries with a nice sharp stick so they can push them back or pop them altogether. When the comic writer hears a little voice in his or her head that says, "That's too much, you shouldn't go there and say *that,*" is when they know they are on the right track.

It can be a good exercise for the writer to "go there" and keep pushing. You never know what comedy gold you might find. Once again, let's consider the success of *South Park*. It pushes the boundaries harder than nearly anything has in the past or the present. Chances are good that Trey and Matt are on a first-name basis with censors who keep telling them to tame it down a bit.

Be Original

Nobody likes a joke thief, and in the small and close-knit world of comedy, it's a surefire way for a lazy comedian or writer to get on the blacklist quickly. Writers and comedians all have influences, but they must all come up with original work that expounds upon those things that have come before.

Tell Personal Stories

When you tell stories that come from a personal place, even if they are highly exaggerated, it can give the audience a chance to empathize with you, and that can make the jokes land even harder. When you are telling personal stories, you are often getting closer to the tragedy of the matter, the place from which so much comedy originates. This is what really gets the audience to empathize.

Not all of the stories need to be true; they just need to *seem* as though they could have happened. Personal stories can be great no matter the form of writing.

Surprise!

The secret to humor is surprise, and really, that's about as close to a unifying theory as you can probably get. Most humor has some type of surprise as a major component. Plays on words, misdirection and misleading setups, and even observational humor all rely on surprise as the joke.

The goal of a writer should be to surprise the audience, and the first step in surprising the audience is surprising the writer. If the writer creates a joke or a scene, and didn't see the exact punch line coming before they got there, that means that most of the time the audience won't see it coming either, and that's when the laughter arrives.

Don't Fear the Absurd

Sometimes, there needs to be a bit of absurdity and surrealism in writing and comedy to make certain types of jokes work. Depending on the style of the comedy, absurdity can work quite well. Farce, for example, can thrive with the absurd, as can parody, as long as the parody still does a good job of mimicking the original.

People don't expect the absurd, and that's one of the best ways of really surprising them.

See How Comedy Writing Works in a Team Setting

Many comedy writers actually work with a partner, and sometimes even in a group setting. On sketch shows and sitcoms, teams of writers come together to create a common vision. A great example of the writer's room is *Six Days to Air*, which gives viewers a behind the scenes look at what it takes to create the show *South Park*. The documentary gives viewers an inside look into the writer's room.

Writers Can't Please Everyone

They shouldn't try to please everyone, either. They just need to make sure they are writing the best original material possible, and they need to find it funny. The subjectivity of humor means that some audiences won't laugh, and that's a natural and normal part of any comedy piece.

Writers should also be willing to keep working on and editing a joke, sketch, or script until they are fully satisfied with it. If the writer or team is happy, it should be able to find an audience.

Writers Keep Writing, Stand-ups Keep Standing Up

Few things in the world are easy, and few people know this better than writers and comics who try to make their living from what is, basically, the handouts of others. If their work is not up to par, the hands that feed them will go away.

Always be writing and always be looking for new and better ideas to use. Most writers will have some type of writing implement with them at all times. Whether you are carrying a stone tablet and chisel, a pen and notebook, or the writer just types his or her missives into a smart phone, it's important to have a place to capture all that genius that finds its way in amidst the crud.

That's right; most of the time, the writing and the jokes just aren't up to par the first time. It takes rewriting, editing, and sometimes scrapping the idea entirely in order to find something that does work.

The only way to get good enough to have a sustainable career as a comedy writer or a stand-up comic is to keep at it. Keep writing and improving on material, change material that doesn't work, and find what does. Find the right voice and the right audience, and that makes it much easier to find success.

Chapter 16

The Thin Line Between Comedy and Tragedy Keeps on Going

These things go together better than chocolate and peanut butter, better than Ben and Jerry, better than unemployment and episodes of *Judge Judy*. This is very evident in most types of humor today, and it is even evident in the real world, without a bit of exaggeration involved, as you will see in a bit.

Look at all of the different types of jokes and comedy out there today. You can easily trace them back to the tragic source in most cases.

Someone falls. It's funny because they fell, and their falling was the tragedy.

Jokes about breaking up with another person can be funny, but the tragedy from which the humor derived stems from the heartbreak. We've all been there and we all know just how it feels too, so we feel empathy for the person telling the story. Yet, we have just enough emotional disconnect to find it humorous.

Look at other types of jokes – except puns and wordplay – and start looking for the tragedy. Chances are good you will find it.

Tragedy is almost omnipresent in humor today, and it has always been that way, all the way back to the Greeks and even those cave people chuckling and slapping their knees when their poor, gaseous friends farted.

In the next section, you'll see a perfect example of this comedy/tragedy connection.

The Headline Says Everything You Need to Know About Tragedy and Comedy

Read this headline and you will laugh and grimace at the same time you realize just what a real tragedy it was. You will likely laugh too because of the irony and because of your psychological distance from the subject. What it all boils down to is that tragedy and comedy are Siamese twins.

The following is a true story. It is sad story too. But you can see it in your mind's eye and you laugh once you read it. People really are terrible.

Here's the headline:

Tycoon Who Took over Segway Dies in a Freak Accident as He Rides One of the Machines off a Cliff and into a River

Conclusion

By now, you should have a much better idea of what comedy is and even why we laugh at certain things and not at others.

Comedy can be a tricky thing, and it really is difficult to define, just as we said earlier. Check out all of the great properties in Chapter 14 and see what makes you laugh and what makes you cringe. That will help to broaden your horizons of humor and even give you a better idea of what is and is not funny, at least to your mind.

Understand the basics of all the theories we've discussed through the book, but it's probably not in your best interest to create a slavish devotion to any one of them. We've already mentioned how none of them is a complete and unified theory of humor. They only touch on the parts of comedy that the creators of the theory find funny for the most part.

By learning about how writers and comedians create jokes and stories, it can help to give you a behind-the-scenes look into the creation of comedy. You might even want to start creating some of your own jokes and humorous stories with the tools and techniques you find in the book.

Just don't be mad when not everyone laughs at your masterpiece. Even though you may follow the "rules" of what you feel is funny, not everyone will find it quite so chuckle-worthy, but that's okay. Do you know why it is okay? In case you haven't heard, since we've only covered it about a million times, humor is… subjective. Just do what makes you laugh. Just make sure you are careful doing it.

Don't Ruin the Joke

As you try to unravel the mystery of humor, you may want to heed the advice of many comedians out there. Learn enough to know how to construct jokes and understand humor, and how to use different techniques to make things funny for particular audiences. However, unless you are a researcher, don't look *too* deeply, and don't try to dissect all of the jokes and everything that makes you laugh. If you do, it yanks away all of the magic that made it funny in the first place.

One of the best things about studying humor and comedy is that you will have a great time doing it. Keep looking for the funny and you are sure to find it!

Glossary

Ad-lib – Making up a joke on the spot. This is not the same as improve, though, since the ad-lib happens with scripted television and movies.

Anecdotal – Comedy that utilizes stories and anecdotes from a person's life to find humor. These anecdotes will generally have a basis in truth, but will also contain some exaggeration to make them funnier.

Benign Violation Theory – The theory states that in order for something to be funny, there needs to be a violation or threat simultaneously seen as benign. This is almost identical to a theory proposed by Thomas Veatch.

Black comedy – This is dark humor, gallows humor, and it is not something everyone enjoys. Subjects for this type of comedy might include depression, suicide, cheating, and all the darker aspects of life.

Blue comedy – This is the place from which all the dirty jokes stem. Blue humor can cover a range of topics, but most of them include subjects that many consider taboo, such as race and sex.

Callback – This is a type of joke that refers to another joke that was told earlier in the comedian's set or earlier in the show or movie. Many comedians will have several callbacks throughout their set, which can help to give it a nice and cohesive feeling.

Dopamine – The chemical the brain releases when we find something funny and laugh. The chemical gives us pleasure, which is why people like to laugh.

Farce – In a farce, things are ridiculous and they simply get more ridiculous as the story or the movie progresses.

FMRI – Functional magnetic resonance imaging machine. Researchers are using this machine to look at the brain patterns and changes to those patterns as people listen to jokes and watch sitcoms.

Improv – Improvisational comedy takes place in real-time with the actor or actors developing and creating comedic stories out of locations, situations, occupations, and more. It is one of the most difficult forms of comedy to master, as it requires fast thinking and working as a team.

Incongruity Theory – The basis of this theory is the unexpected brings humor. You give people one thing and then hit them with something completely different, but which still makes sense.

Observational comedy – This type of comedy comes from the observations made by the comedian about the normal goings on of everyday life, often exaggerated for a more comedic effect.

Mechanical Theory – This is a subset of the Superiority Theory, and it relies on humor coming from rigidity and the lack of change in a person, even though everyone around the person can see he or she needs to be more flexible and needs to make changes in life.

Parody – This is imitation of another work and the intent of the parody is to make light of or ridicule the original property.

Physical comedy – this type of comedy is not subtle and utilizes falls, making silly faces, tripping and stumbling, and walking into walls as humor. It's is an old style of comedy and is popular with clowns. It is very much the same as slapstick comedy, just under a different name.

Pratfall – A type of physical comedy where the performer actually falls down in order to elicit laughter from the audience. Many comic actors, including John Ritter, have used this form of humor successfully. Ritter's character name on the show *Three's Company* was Jack Tripper, and with a name like that, you know the guy was probably going to fall down a lot.

Prop comics – These comedians literally use props as a major part of their act. Perhaps the most popular of the prop comedians working today is Carrot Top.

Relief/Release Theory – A theory posed by Freud, among others, that states humor is a way to release psychic or mental energy through laughter. They felt that humor relied on the tension-relief model.

Satire – Satire mocks the weaknesses and problems in society and in humans in general. Political satire, such as is seen on *The Daily Show*, is probably one of the most common forms you will see.

Sarcasm – Makes fun of a person or of a situation, often at the expense of that person's feelings. Sarcasm can sometimes be quite cruel. Some feel that this is a low form of humor.

Sitcom – A situational comedy on television. Prominent examples of this from today and yesterday include *The Cosby Show*, *Two and a Half Men*, *The Big Bang Theory*, and *The Andy Griffith Show*.

Slapstick – Tripping, falling, slipping, and getting hit in the face with pies all fall into this category, which is still present on television and in film even though it is not as prominent as it once was.

Stand-up – This is where a comedian will literally stand up in front of a crowd and tell jokes that are a part of his or her routine. Comedians have different types of routines that can contain a host of different elements.

Superiority Theory – The basis behind this theory is that people will laugh whenever they feel superior to another person or even when they feel superior over a situation, an idea or ideal, a political situation, and more. Plato, Hobbes, and other philosophers championed this idea.

Surreal – This comedy takes turns that do not often make much sense in reality, although the punch lines can really land when done properly. A good example would be deadpan, surreal comedian

Steven Wright's joke about owning a paranoid retriever dog. When he throws something, the dog brings back *everything* because he's just not sure what was thrown and doesn't want to be wrong.

Resources:

http://skullsinthestars.com/2007/10/03/the-link-between-horror-and-comedy-and-the-best-horrorcomedy-films/

http://www.thinctanc.co.uk/words/comedy.html

http://standupcomedysecrets.blogspot.com/2013/06/is-all-stand-up-comedy-material-based.html

http://humorinamerica.wordpress.com/2013/04/18/standing-askew-if-tragedy-plus-time-equals-comedy-what-do-you-call-it-when-there-is-no-time/

http://www.dead-frog.com/comedians/best_delivery

http://www.humorpower.com/art-rulethree.html

http://listverse.com/2011/10/31/top-10-great-satirists/

http://mentalfloss.com/article/27575/10-parody-novels-get-last-laugh

http://comedyknockout.com/history-slapstick

http://en.wikipedia.org/wiki/The_Benny_Hill_Show

http://comedians.about.com/od/top10lists/tp/Five-Most-Sarcastic-Comedians.htm

http://www.listal.com/movies/farce/2/all

http://voices.yahoo.com/the-roots-surrealist-comedy-11424690.html?cat=2

http://listverse.com/2008/12/15/top-10-brilliant-black-comedies/

http://nakedspeaker.com/2012/04/16/what-is-improv-comedy/

http://www.pantheater.com/articles-rules-of-improv-part-i-improv-comedy.html

http://thelaughbutton.com/features/laugh-guide-blue-humor/

http://science.howstuffworks.com/life/laughter.htm

http://www.dailywritingtips.com/20-types-and-forms-of-humor/

http://science.howstuffworks.com/life/inside-the-mind/human-brain/formula-for-funny.htm

http://www.psychologytoday.com/articles/200011/the-science-laughter

http://myweb.brooklyn.liu.edu/jlyttle/Humor/Theory.htm

http://www.pragmaticshumour.net/makingsenseofhumour/1.1superiority_theories.htm

http://www.pragmaticshumour.net/makingsenseofhumour/1.3incongruity_theories.htm

http://www.pragmaticshumour.net/makingsenseofhumour/1.2relief_theories.htm

http://blogs.psychcentral.com/humor/2012/07/do-you-laugh-when-some-one-falls-is-it-a-superiority-theory-or-fact-of-life/

https://www.msu.edu/~jdowell/monro.html

http://pov.imv.au.dk/Issue_26/section_1/artc8A.html

http://www.academia.edu/477378/Humor_Theories_and_the_Physiological_Benefits_of_Laughter

http://www.richardwiseman.com/LaughLab/incon.html

http://www.3quarksdaily.com/3quarksdaily/2011/02/paradigm-shifts-in-art-humor-and-science.html

http://magazine.hearts2.com/read~article-why-do-we-laugh~a-171~pp-up.html?pp_do=print

http://www.wired.com/magazine/2011/04/ff_humorcode/

http://www.drwrite.com/SNHU/344/docs/theories.shtml

http://digitalcommons.unl.edu/cgi/viewcontent.cgi?article=1010&context=englishunsllc

http://www.timoroso.com/philosophy/writings/sketches/2006-04-09-henri-bergsons-theory-of-laughter

http://leeds-faculty.colorado.edu/mcgrawp/Benign_Violation_Theory.html

http://thewritepractice.com/the-very-worst-missionarys-four-tips-of-being-funny/

http://blog.petermcgraw.org/2010/09/a-brief-introduction-to-the-benign-violation-theory-of-humor/

http://www.metafilter.com/95188/The-Benign-Violation-Theory-of-humor-from-HuRL

http://www.tomveatch.com/else/humor/summary.9907.html

http://www.humanities360.com/index.php/the-relief-theory-and-its-effect-on-humor-65170/

http://www.iep.utm.edu/humor/

http://www.drbarbaramaier.at/shiblesw/humorbook/h8%20theory.html

http://www.lebed.com/HumorTheory/HumorTheoryfinal1.htm

http://www.wikihow.com/Use-Humor-As-a-Defense-Mechanism

http://www.dailystrength.org/health_blogs/cyndi/article/the-anatomy-of-sarcasm-is-it-real-humor-or-just-someones-defense-mechanism

http://drsanity.blogspot.com/2004/08/psychiatry-101-defense-mechanisms.html

http://theoncologist.alphamedpress.org/content/10/8/651.full

http://www.yadvashem.org/yv/en/education/conference/2004/55.pdf

http://www.articlesbase.com/humor-articles/the-evolution-of-comedy-758800.html

http://flavorwire.com/412175/the-50-funniest-movies-ever-made/view-all/

http://splitsider.com/2013/02/the-ultimate-comedy-library-54-books-every-comedy-fan-should-read/

http://www.clydepark.com/history.htm

http://yubanet.com/oddnews/100-Funniest-Words-in-English.php#.Un2cQPnUBsI

http://www.chortle.co.uk/correspondents/2013/05/13/17841/15_tips_for_new_comedy_writers

http://scribemeetsworld.com/2011/screenplay-writing/how-to-write-a-comedy-script-screenwriting-tips-hangover/

http://www.writersdigest.com/whats-new/10-ways-to-improve-your-writing-while-thinking-like-a-comedy-writer

http://darkcargo.com/2013/04/29/five-practical-tips-on-writing-humor-by-alex-shvartsman/

http://www.krisneri.com/tips2.html

http://annastan.livejournal.com/25384.html

http://writetodone.com/how-to-write-funny/

http://writeworld.tumblr.com/post/46133265223/nine-tips-on-writing-humor-from-scott-adams

http://worddreams.wordpress.com/2013/07/08/10-tips-for-comedy-writers/

http://www.humorpower.com/blog/2006/04/41-tips-for-writing-funny-lines/

Photo Credits

In order of appearance:

http://commons.wikimedia.org/wiki/File:Felix_Cat-Haha_%28transp_sharp%29.png

http://commons.wikimedia.org/wiki/File:Tales_of_Horror_01.jpg

http://commons.wikimedia.org/wiki/File:Abbott_and_Costello_Meet_F
http://commons.wikimedia.org/wiki/File:Louis_CK_Kuwait_crop_cropped.jpgrankenstein_Logo.png

http://commons.wikimedia.org/wiki/File:Jack_Klugman_Tony_Randall_The_Odd_Couple_1972.JPG

http://commons.wikimedia.org/wiki/File:Brian_Posehn_Get_Smart_premiere_arrival.jpg

http://commons.wikimedia.org/wiki/File:Brian_Posehn_Get_Smart_premiere_arrival.jpg

http://upload.wikimedia.org/wikipedia/commons/0/0f/Dane_Cook_Co

http://upload.wikimedia.org/wikipedia/commons/2/2d/Kyle-cassidy-weird-al-yankovic.jpgmicCon.*JPG*

http://upload.wikimedia.org/wikipedia/commons/a/aa/Stephen_Colbert_and_Army_Chief_of_Staff_Gen._Raymond_T._Odierno_pay_tribute_to_the_homecoming_troops_of_the_Iraq_war_with_an_a_cappella_rendition_of_%22I%27ll_Be_Home_for_Christmas%22_during_the_recording_of_the_Colbert_Report.jpg

http://commons.wikimedia.org/wiki/File:Bob_Odenkirk_2013.jpg

http://commons.wikimedia.org/wiki/File:Turpin-Ben_05.jpg

http://commons.wikimedia.org/wiki/File:Mabel_Normand_card.jpg

http://commons.wikimedia.org/wiki/File:Three%27s_Company_roommates_1977.JPG

http://upload.wikimedia.org/wikipedia/commons/7/75/Dick_Van_Dyke_Petrie_family_1963.JPG

http://commons.wikimedia.org/wiki/File:KeystoneKops.jpg

http://commons.wikimedia.org/wiki/File:Daniel_Tosh_at_Boston_Univ
http://commons.wikimedia.org/wiki/File:Sarahsilvermangfdl.PNGersity.jpg

http://commons.wikimedia.org/wiki/File:Duck_Soup_2.jpg

http://commons.wikimedia.org/wiki/File:SteveCoogan1SecondFilm.jpg

http://commons.wikimedia.org/wiki/File:Russell_Brand_Arthur_Premier_mike.jpg

http://commons.wikimedia.org/wiki/File:Dave_Attell_2009.jpg

http://commons.wikimedia.org/wiki/File:Jim_Gaffigan_Performing_at_Carolines10_crop.jpg

http://commons.wikimedia.org/wiki/File:AlexanderBain001.jpg

http://commons.wikimedia.org/wiki/File:Henri_Bergson_(Nobel).jpg

http://commons.wikimedia.org/wiki/File:Immanuel_Kant_2.jpg

http://commons.wikimedia.org/wiki/File:Spencer1.jpg

http://commons.wikimedia.org/wiki/File:Carrol_O%27Connor_as_Archie_Bunker.JPG

http://commons.wikimedia.org/wiki/File:Dr._Strangelove_-_The_War_Room.png

http://commons.wikimedia.org/wiki/File:Jimmy_Durante_in_Broadway_to_Hollywood_trailer.jpg

http://commons.wikimedia.org/wiki/File:The_Three_Stooges_1962.JPG

All photos are licensed under Creative Commons and free to share and remix as long as the new product is also made available to share alike.